Achieving

QTS

D1635386

Learning to Teach

Primary PE

Achieving QTS

Learning to Teach
Primary PE

**Ian Pickup, Lawry Price,
Julie Shaughnessy, Jon Spence
and Maxine Trace**

LearningMatters

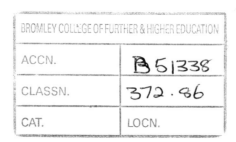
First published in 2008 by Learning Matters Ltd.

British Library Cataloguing in Publication Data
A CIP record for this book is available from the British Library.

ISBN: 978 1 84445 142 5

Cover design by Topics; text design by Code 5 Design Associates Ltd
Project management by Deer Park Productions, Tavistock
Typeset by PDQ Typesetting Ltd, Newcastle under Lyme
Printed and bound in Great Britain by Cromwell Press Ltd, Trowbridge, Wiltshire
Learning Matters
33 Southernhay East
Exeter EX1 1NX
Tel: 01392 215560
info@learningmatters.co.uk
www.learningmatters.co.uk

Contents

About the authors

Ian Pickup

Ian Pickup is currently Director of Sport and Wellbeing at Roehampton University, having previously been Principal Lecturer and Subject Leader in physical education. Before joining Roehampton, Ian taught in secondary and primary schools, and within further education, worked as a development officer for the Rugby Football Union and played professional rugby. Ian is currently conducting research into the physical self-perception of trainee teachers and is a partner within an EU-funded project focusing on physical education in the early years. He has recently published *Teaching Physical Education in the Primary School: A Developmental Approach* (Continuum; with Lawry Price) and was awarded a National Teaching Fellowship by the Higher Education Academy in 2007.

Lawry Price

Lawry Price is Assistant Dean (Learning and Teaching) and Principal Lecturer in Physical Education in the School of Education at Roehampton University. He has co- and single-authored four publications in the field of physical education and presented research papers at both national and international conferences. This collaboration brings to bear the expertise of a team of colleagues committed to a developmental approach to teaching the subject of physical education in primary schools, a personal philosophy that has underpinned 30 years of practice and teaching the subject across all age groups from toddlers to octogenarians.

Julie Shaughnessy

Julie Shaughnessy is EdD Programme Director and a Principal Lecturer in the School of Education at Roehampton University. At Roehampton she has developed a range of courses and resources for primary physical education to support initial teacher education and continuing professional development.

Jon Spence

Jon Spence has over 20 years' experience as a teacher, mentor and lecturer working in a variety of schools, sixth form colleges and in higher education. Jon is currently Enterprise Manager of the Roehampton Consortium, a tutor on the National Continuing Professional Development programme and Regional Coordinator for Physical Education Initial Teacher Training in London and the South East. A passionate physical educationalist Jon's particular research interest, and the focus of his PhD, is the importance of teamwork and the ways in which it can be developed to improve performance.

Maxine Trace

Maxine Trace spent six years employed as a classroom teacher and Physical Education Subject Leader in a south west London primary school before starting work as a Senior Lecturer in Physical Education in the School of Education at Roehampton University. Maxine teaches both BA and PGCE primary physical education modules for subject specialists and generalist trainees, and a separate course for Return to Teaching students. Part of her role is also dedicated to supervising students' block school experience across the academic year and to providing CPD opportunities to schools in neighbouring local authorities. Maxine co-authored and presented a paper at Roehampton's ROERCE 2 conference in December 2005 and has had work published in the British Journal of Teaching Physical Education (BJTPE) (Spring 2006, Vol. 37, No.10).

Introduction

It is not the first intention of this book to inform you about how to teach physical education successfully to primary aged children. However, it is an aim for all readers to be encouraged in the pursuit of teaching the subject effectively, with enthusiasm, and with an ever developing understanding of the subject's worth and place in the primary curriculum. To this end therefore we address the content of this book to all practising teachers, be they at the very beginning of their career working towards Qualified Teacher Status, or those who aspire to attain Excellent Teacher or to become Advanced Skills Teachers – the premise being that there is always more we can learn about doing the job better.

The team of writers who have contributed to the contents of this book hold firm to the principles embedded within teaching physical education developmentally. The provision of physical learning experiences that are conducive to the growth and development of the individual child is key to this and that is why an advocacy for a model of professional practice which is based on personal reflection and self-appraisal is the central theme of the book. We have therefore intentionally included practical and reflective tasks to complete that facilitate this growth in professional practice, by identifying specific teaching characteristics which underpin the 'good practice' examples throughout each chapter.

Each chapter makes a significant contribution to helping support the key objectives of providing quality physical education learning. Chapter 1 sets a context for the subject and highlights the benefits of learning in physical education for children and crucially too for teachers. Chapter 2 provides a seam of potential physical education content from which effective planning, teaching and assessment can ensure a rich learning experience for the children in our charge. Chapter 3 addresses the structure and function of the Professional Standards for Teachers, how they relate directly to physical education, and how evidence can be accumulated to meet such requirements. Chapter 4 looks at contemporary debate, research and issues within primary physical education including references to the Primary National Strategy, *Excellence and Enjoyment* and the *Every Child Matters* agendas. In Chapter 5 the importance of health and safety considerations is fully addressed with guidelines for good practice included, and throughout there are references to support teaching and learning in physical education for the primary age phase.

We hope you will enjoy reading the contents of this book, at whatever stage in your teaching career you find yourself. Our wish is that this book makes a contribution of marked quality to the profession generally, but most of all that is significant in supporting those who value and identify with the medium of learning through the physical domain as a key to unlocking children's natural enthusiasms and motivations. Please, above all else, *enjoy* – which might reflect most accurately what we want our children to get out of their own physical education experiences.

Ian Pickup
Lawry Price
Julie Shaughnessy
Jon Spence
Maxine Trace

March 2008

1

The importance of physical education in primary schools
Lawry Price

> **By the end of this chapter you will have an understanding of:**
>
> - the status and importance of physical education;
> - the benefits of physical education for children and teachers;
> - knowledge about what constitutes quality physical education;
> - how developing a personal rationale and philosophy for the teaching of physical education informs the effective teaching of the subject.
>
> This chapter addresses, and makes a contribution to, the following Professional Standards for QTS:
>
> - **Professional attributes – Q1, Q2, Q4, Q5, Q6, Q7, Q8, Q9**
> - **Professional knowledge and understanding – Q10, Q18**
> - **Professional skills – Q29, Q32, Q33**

Introduction

The importance of physical education: What does the subject provide for learners?

Why do we teach what we are required to teach?

Alongside informed notions about what we believe children need *to know* and should be able *to do*, teachers will draw from their own personal knowledge base to establish the principles and values upon which they build a personal philosophy for their own teaching. This inevitably changes and develops over time as further knowledge and experience accrue and contribute to allow us to become the rounded *professional* we all aspire to at the beginning of our teaching careers.

When it comes to considering specifically why we teach physical education there may well be less existent informed knowledge, although primary practitioners will commit to educating the *whole* child as a foundation principle of their everyday practice. Looking at this from a child's perspective there is little doubt that general movement and physical activity play a centrally important role in the lives of children and young people. Bailey (2001) illustrates this graphically in his research findings, pointing out the following as barometers for the subject's importance.

- Physical activity play is the first appearing and most frequently occurring expression of play in infants.
- Children in all cultures around the world engage in spontaneous and rule-governed forms of physical activity.

- Most children would rather take part in physical activities than in any other endeavour.
- They would also prefer to succeed in those activities than in classroom-based work.
- Physical competence is a major factor influencing social acceptance in children of all ages and both sexes.
- Regular physical activity can make significant positive contributions to the physical, mental and emotional well-being of children.

The status and importance of physical education are spelt out in National Curriculum and QCA documentation and above all else emphasise its unique place in the curriculum as the only area of learning that focuses on the body, its constituent parts, and the development of its movement potential.

When this is set alongside the physical development learning area noted in the *Curriculum Guidance for the Early Years Foundation Stage*, and numerous references contained within the texts, books and teaching resources that support the teaching of the subject, we can begin to appreciate more fully both the subject's pronounced importance and its uniqueness.

First and foremost, PE supports and develops individual children's physical competence, and by doing so their self-esteem and personal confidence. The motor skills acquired through effective teaching and learning serve the purpose of helping children to perform in a variety of physical pursuits, not just in a school setting but also for everyday activity, and such skills prepare them for the practical physical demands of their daily lives.

By promoting physical skillfulness, physical development and a growing knowledge of the body in action, PE provides opportunities within its activities frameworks for children to be creative and expressive, to experience competition and to take on challenges as individuals, or in groups or teams.

Additionally, and perhaps most significantly, PE promotes positive attitudes towards active and healthy lifestyles, and clearly contributes to lifelong participation in activity as part of staying fit and healthy. Through such a process of learning children can discover their own unique aptitudes, abilities and personal preferences, and thereby can make informed choices about how they can get involved in lifelong physical activity.

When all of this is set against the particular learning needs of children within the 3–11 school setting, it is clear that there exists a multiplicity of benefits for pupils and teachers alike from quality physical education provision.

But all of this depends on the subject being well taught, and this is where you as the teacher can have a significant impact so that children are highly motivated and approach their learning in the subject enthusiastically, and with a continuing yearning and desire to perform to the best of their abilities.

Some recent developments in the world of PE have been:

- World Summit – Magglingen (Switzerland, 2005);
- UK – afPE Mission Statement (revised 2006);
- National strategies – PESSCL/CPD;
- New Association – AfPE-defined aims for PE;

- New curriculum developments – *Foundation* and *Formative* Physical Education;
- New standards for the teaching profession extending from training through to AST/Excellent Teacher status;
- *Every Child Matters* agenda.

Starting points

The term *physical education* conjures up a range of thoughts and emotions dependent upon your own personal experience. These can vary from the positive vibe of the benefits accrued from such learning experiences in school to the downright negative view of painful memories that include exposure to the elements and performing in front of others.

Whatever your experience, there is a statutory obligation for the entitlement of children to receive a physical education of relevance, usefulness, value and quality. Standing back and reflecting on what the outcome of this *not* happening will be opens a debate about the *whole* education of the child – clearly an important and significant component would be missing if such learning opportunities were not provided.

As a teacher you will be uniquely placed in the primary school setting to oversee all aspects of individual children's development and will be responsible for their intellectual, spiritual, moral, social and physical development during this period of compulsory education. Advocacy for a *developmental* approach to the teaching of physical education, which emphasises the focus on each individual child's needs, is crucial within this philosophy for the subject. This necessitates ensuring that the PE experiences that are provided are appropriate and take full account of children's psychomotor, cognitive, social and emotional development during the primary stages of learning.

As a teacher of physical education you will need a clear picture of what you are helping children to achieve in this area of the curriculum. If the definition of *becoming physically educated* includes mastering motor skills, being physically fit, regularly participating in physical activity, understanding the benefits and risks of physical activity, possessing a knowledge about a range of activities that entail physical activity, and valuing physical activity as a lifelong pursuit, then ensuring it is developmentally appropriate for the individual (that is always putting individual needs first in a sensitive and supportive teaching–learning environment) is of the essence. Above all a recognition that herein lies an important part of children's overall education is vital and indeed crucial to that premise.

Within the *Every Child Matters* agenda there is further testimony that physical education has a significant role to play in the fulfillment and delivery of the five outcomes noted in the strategy, central as they are to education's role in society. The five outcomes are as follows.

- Being healthy: enjoying good physical and mental health and living a healthy lifestyle.
- Staying safe: being protected from harm and neglect.
- Enjoying and achieving: getting the most out of life and developing the skills for adulthood.
- Making a positive contribution: being involved in the community and society and not engaging in antisocial or offensive behaviour.
- Economic well-being: not being prevented by economic disadvantage from achieving full potential in life.

Your responsibilities in these aspects can clearly take physical education as a key contributor to achieving these defined outcomes.

REFLECTIVE TASK

Learning objective: to recall your own personal physical education

What can you remember about your own experiences of engaging in physical education activity when you were in primary school?

Can you recall working with hoops, bean bags, quoits, skipping-ropes, and airflow balls in games activities?

Can you remember doing country dancing and dreading holding hands for the first time with a member of the opposite sex?!

Have you memories about working on gymnastic apparatus structures, attempting to climb ropes and experiencing the thrill of the extra spring you could get from using a beat-board?

Remember playground games and playing in teams? Remember *Rounders*?

Do you remember sports days? What particular features of such events stick out in your mind?

Make notes against each of the questions posed above and use as a possible set of starting points for developing your own philosophy for the subject.

Benefits of PE for children

Understanding the range of benefits that a quality physical education experience gives children is of paramount importance in constructing a personal rationale for the subject, particularly its contribution to an individual child's quality of life. These include:

- physical fitness;
- psychomotor skills;
- regular physical activity;
- emotional well-being;
- social skills;
- personal responsibility;
- cognitive skills;
- subject-related knowledge.

The first and perhaps most obvious benefit (but always worth stating and emphasising) is *physical fitness*. Children possess an innate need to move, even from their very first moments of coming into the world, and with opportunity and encouragement from siblings, parents and adults (not least teachers) they will be physically fit as a result of their PE in school and the other range of movement activities they engage in out of school. Physical education makes a contribution to building individual children's overall endurance capabilities, but it also involves cardio-respiratory fitness work, supporting the growth in muscular strength that occurs during the primary age phase, muscular endurance for a range of different activities, the maintenance of flexibility, and body composition emphasis (the rate of body fat mass to lean tissue mass). When considering these crucial components of physical fitness we are defining *health-related fitness* as opposed to *sport-* or *skill-related physical fitness* which involves the specific skills and strengths needed to excel at a particular sport. School-based physical education should endeavour to ensure that children benefit from a broad approach to physical fitness that aims to encourage a lifelong commitment for physical health, not just sport-specific mastery.

A second benefit is the systematic and progressive learning of *psychomotor skills*. It can come as a shock, and sometimes will raise eyebrows, that physical skills are not innate, do not develop naturally, and that we need (and indeed benefit) from learning these in a planned and progressive way, noting along the way how important it is to learn *how* to learn new skills. A planned, logical and sequenced learning cycle will provide children with the basic motor concepts and skills that they can apply both within the physical education setting itself and beyond. The skills required, for example, for block building in a nursery setting are applicable to the grasp needed to manipulate bean bags and quoits in PE, with hand–eye coordination learnt in one context transferred to another albeit for a different purpose. Highlighting PE's contribution to life skills, beyond the practical skills learning it provides, is a powerful justification for its inclusion on schools curricula.

The need for *regular physical activity* is manifest when health is discussed. Coming behind smoking, high blood pressure, and high cholesterol, physical inactivity is the fourth most prevalent risk factor for coronary heart disease in the western world. Without discounting the value of children's own playtime and their personal choice of recreational pursuits as opportunities to exercise, the provision of regular, scheduled, physical education will provide children with the benefits of regular physical activity. For some children this may well be their only chance to exercise in a meaningful way, deriving in the course of it the benefits of structured learning. It may well be that this is a rare chance for children's heart rates to increase and where they can involve themselves in vigorous warm ups and cool downs, and respond to instructions to induce amounts of physical activity. Additionally PE lessons and experiences that are conducted in a way that promotes further interest and commitment to physical activity in out-of-school contexts are to be applauded. If your approach to teaching physical education is characterised by encouraging children to enjoy their physical education, you are more likely to see those beneficiaries pursuing after-school activity and beyond that into later life. This therefore highlights the need to learn basic skills and to be able to perform and enjoy physical activity, to have positive physical activity experiences, and to nurture and further understand the benefits of physical activity. In these ways, children benefit from physical education because they learn to seek physical activity as a way of life.

If physical education promotes physical activity as a way of life, it also promotes *emotional well-being*. Research indicates that those who exercise regularly are less likely to feel depressed or anxious (USDHHS, 1997). This suggests they are more likely to enjoy psychological well-being. Additionally, engaging in positive physical activity experiences can enhance significantly the personal confidence and self-esteem, particularly that of children who are primarily kinesthetic learners. Such positive experiences combine to benefit the rest of the curriculum as children who are feeling good about themselves will act and behave positively across the board, more ready and in the right frame of mind to learn in all areas.

Physical education teaches, develops and reinforces *social skills*. Activities such as making up games which harness and test out newly-learnt skills with a group of fellow pupils, commenting on a partner's gymnastics sequence, or problem solving within a team to outwit opponents tactically in a team challenge, all require social skills that in turn can be used in other school experiences and daily lives. The practice of accepting others' physical abilities and limitations and of working as members of groups and teams to enhance each individual's success can lend itself to accepting diversity and difference in other school settings. In a supportive teaching and learning environment children can develop and hone social skills potentially as much, if not more, in the PE setting as in the regular classroom. PE can provide the perfect arena in which to develop social skills.

Children's ability increasingly to take *personal responsibility* for themselves is as marked in physical education as in other areas of the curriculum. As children acquire knowledge and fuller understanding as well as greater physical competence, they can gradually assume more and more personal responsibility for their physical well-being and their activities in and stemming from the physical education setting. This will lead to an acceptance of trying out the new activities that are introduced to them, a greater involvement in out-of-school activity, and a willingness to work with anyone in their class setting – all traits of growing personal responsibility and self-motivation for learning.

If a problem-solving and questioning approach is taken with regard to physical education teaching, as advocated within a developmental model, it is then a logical step to engage children cognitively. Asking children to make up a game using racket skills, or setting a challenge to discover ways of balancing on three parts of the body, or to respond movement-wise to a series of particular sounds, rhythms and beats, will all enhance *cognitive skills*. Physical activity therefore enhances academic learning and achievement across the curriculum through a focus on body movement that both reinforces and extends the habit of problem solving as a learning tool.

All of the above inform us of the benefits that an effective physical education programme brings to children. This *knowledge* goes with them beyond the PE setting itself, and, in addition gives them insight into the specific benefits of physical activity, the particular risks that participation in certain activities have, and how to minimise the chance of injury. Finally, through physical education, children learn about the risks of inactivity, and the importance of physical fitness for an active and healthy lifestyle.

Benefits of PE for teachers

It can be stated categorically that the benefits of PE are not just for the children in our care. As a teacher you will also benefit in a variety of personal and professional ways, not least through the regular scheduling and teaching of PE lessons, because the subject can contribute to making classroom management and the implicit assessment required easier to handle. It might even offer opportunities for you to exercise on a regular basis as well!

Here we will look at the following.

- Enhancing the skills of classroom management.
- An effective means of evaluation and assessment.
- Personal fitness.

Teaching a subject that focuses on body movement clearly facilitates and *enhances the skills of classroom management*. Children, particularly very young ones, do not generally like to sit still or be passive learners, so providing frequent and consistent opportunities to move in purposeful, appropriate and relevant ways brings with them a growing sense of class community and identity and most notably an atmosphere of cooperation. Children benefiting in this respect are more accessible, amenable and ready to learn. However, we should not lose sight of the fact that movement opportunities do not come alone from PE experiences – drama (role play, dance, general body control) and science (work on balance, healthy bodies, levers, and so on) will draw on PE movement concepts and vice versa.

The teaching of movement activities will give you *an effective means of evaluation and assessment* for other subjects. PE is a subject where there is immediate detection of a shortfall of understanding and feedback on response to task because it is visually discernible – you don't have to collect a book in to confirm understanding – the evidence is there before you! Such strategies can be usefully employed in other learning settings and can supply an extra tool in your box of strategies for dealing with the challenges of assessment.

Last, but by no means least, an acceptance of the principle that teachers can (and do!) learn with and alongside the children in their classes further illustrates the benefits of including PE in the curriculum. Here is your chance to join in physically with the children in their learning, even accepting you are learning alongside and together with your pupils. This models your own stand on the importance of PE and the need to try, even if it's difficult and you are not good at it either! Children's general reaction to this is usually encouraging and supportive and the bottom line might be that your *personal fitness* is maintained as a result!

REFLECTIVE TASK

Good practice principles

What therefore is *good physical education*? As an exercise it is worth considering the following 13 features that an individual school might present as a model of quality physical education provision.

1   The school has an up-to-date and recently-reviewed policy for the teaching of the subject that reflects the practical realities and context and crucially this is put into everyday practice.

2   The school's PE policy has been put together and agreed upon by all members of staff, establishing a principle of 'ownership' of the product. It includes a rationale for the subject's inclusion in the curriculum, frameworks for delivery, reference to safety factors, and an acknowledgement of the importance of teaching codes of health and personal hygiene through the subject.

3   Whether you are teaching *physical development* in the Foundation Stage or *national curriculum PE* for children aged 5–11, facilities and resources are being fully utilised to provide the very best learning opportunities for children, which should include effective deployment of the teaching expertise that resides with individuals on the school staff.

4   There exists a full commitment and rationalised allocation of sufficient time to enable children to maximise their physical development potential, that is reflective of *access and entitlement* principles.

5   There is a whole-school philosophy of physical education in place and an embedded understanding and knowledge of the benefits of the subject to children's all-round development – spiritually, morally, socially, culturally and physically.

6   The plans and schemes of work that are in place ensure the continuity and progression of learning across the areas of activity, and just as importantly, maintain a breadth and balance in the full range of different physical learning experiences.

7   Planning and on-going assessment are integral, and complements where possible (and useful to do so) with related work happening elsewhere in the curriculum.

8   There is a continuous programme of physical education work throughout the primary age-phase (including that of the Foundation Stage) that takes full account of the changing physiological developments and needs of all children.

9 There is a pervading awareness of the need to review practice continually in the light of changing circumstances and continuing staff development opportunities for PE remain on the agenda as much as for all other teaching and learning matters.

10 There is a coordinator for the subject in place to oversee trends and developments, one who is prepared to articulate the subject's particular case – for example in the matters of resources and finance available for curriculum development.

11 There remains a commitment to acknowledging that PE is a unique subject in that it is the only one that focuses on the body and its potential for movement. Because of this premise the subject needs to be taught regularly, consistently, with enthusiasm, and with high expectations of what children can achieve, at the same time allowing children the opportunities to work to the limit of their abilities.

12 Teaching styles allow for a full range of delivery of subject content, from teacher-directed to self-exploration, in keeping and consistent with the strategies employed in day-to-day practice in the classroom.

13 PE lessons are characterised by being lively, active, fun and enjoyable – for children and teachers alike. They are well organised, have a defined purpose, and build on previous knowledge and understanding to create a notion of working towards increased confidence and self-esteem, as well as physical competence – again for children and teachers alike.

Thinking about your current school, or most recent placement, reflect on how PE compares and stands up to the key features of 'good practice principles' above. What areas need particular attention when addressing the challenge of improving the quality of provision within your school?

PRACTICAL TASK PRACTICAL TASK PRACTICAL TASK PRACTICAL TASK PRACTICAL TASK

To add to the conclusions you have drawn from the above exercise conduct an audit against the PE health checklist below. What can you deduce from these two exercises that identifies what needs to happen to improve the overall quality of PE provision within your current, or most recent, school setting?

Reviewing PE in schools – a 'health' checklist of questions

PREMISES

- To what extent does the accommodation facilitate or hinder the delivery of physical education experiences?
- What particular provision is there for physical development opportunities in the Foundation Stage or the areas of activity within National Curriculum frameworks?
- Are indoor spaces sufficiently large and high, the floor surfaces clean, well maintained and appropriately marked, the spaces suitably heated and ventilated, and the surrounds free from potential hazards?
- Are outdoor facilities similarly appropriately marked and maintained? Are they appropriate for the activities for which they are being used?
- Are there adequate/appropriate facilities for storage, changing, first-aid and telephone contact for emergency purposes?

RESOURCES

- Is there a policy for resource management, including the maintenance and replacement of equipment?
- Are there sufficient resources to support the overall school physical education programme (including ones to support teacher planning) and so allow every child to achieve and sustain high standards?

- Are the resources appropriate for the activities and tasks the children's stages of development, as well as sufficient in quantity, variety and quality, and well maintained?

ORGANISATION

- Are there clear policy documentation and curriculum guidelines in place for the delivery of physical education in the school?
- Do the aims for PE link with the school strategic aims and objectives?
- Are there references within the existent policy for PE for curriculum, finance, health and safety, changing provision, staff meetings, staff development, and development planning?

STAFFING

- Are the teachers' professional qualifications appropriate for teaching the subject/activity?
- Are teachers deployed purposefully, effectively and with their strengths, experience and expertise considered?
- Are there appropriate arrangements for the induction of new staff, appraisal and in-service training?
- Are any instructors or coaches employed, and if so are they supervised appropriately?

CURRICULUM

- Does the curriculum provide an appropriate balance of areas of activity and avoid duplication, repetition and overlap? Is there a range of varied opportunities for children to develop a broad physical competence?
- Does the time allocated to each area of activity allow children to experience continuity and progression in skill, knowledge and understanding?
- Does the time allocated to each area of activity allow children to demonstrate their developing skill, knowledge and understanding?
- Do aspects of the PE curriculum link with other areas of the curriculum e.g. Arts, PSHE, Literacy, Numeracy?
- Are whole school policies (e.g. Equal Opportunities, Assessment, Special Needs, *Every Child Matters*) reflected in practice in the PE curriculum?
- Does the PE curriculum demonstrate in planning and practice continuity of approach and curricular progression?

TEACHING AND LEARNING

- Do lessons have a variety of activity and good pace?
- Are there appropriate learning objectives which are shared with the children?
- Is the individual teacher's delivery sensitive to individual needs and particular groupings of children?
- Do children fully engage in the activities offered and is their individual work rate consistent with the demands of the tasks presented?
- Do children exhibit skilful body management, an ability to observe and recall movement, knowledge of movement principles, rules and conventions for the activities in which they are engaged?
- Do children work well as individuals, with partners, in groups and in teams, and show respect for others' ideas and physical abilities, compete fairly and are able to cope with both success and failure?
- Are children given opportunities to plan, undertake and review to inform their future performance?
- Are opportunities included in lessons to provide links with other curriculum areas and incorporate cross-curricular aspects?

ASSESSMENT AND RECORDING

- Are assessment and recording arrangements consistent with the requirements for the Foundation Stage and National Curriculum provision?
- Are assessment and recording linked to learning objectives?
- Are procedures and practice consistent with school policies?
- Are assessment methods appropriate for the age range and abilities of the children and the desired learning objectives?
- Do the results of assessment inform future planning and assist progression?

Developing a personal philosophy or rationale for PE – personal values

CASE STUDY

Trace the story of an active professional, still engaged in physical activity, as presented below. As a personalised Reflective Task consider your own Physical Activity Lifeline. How would you complete a table as depicted, and what particular features stand out for you in determining your own Physical Activity Lifeline Profile?

Follow this up by afterwards reading the Year 2 undergraduate profile.

The changing physical activity lifeline (adapted from Jess, 2004)
An example of a male, in his early 50s, and a physical activity professional

STRAND	Primary school	Secondary school	Early adulthood (18-40)	Mid-adulthood (40-60)
Functional	Lots of walking (no family car) and many buses and trains.	Still lots of walking and use of public transport. Paper rounds and holiday jobs.	Car – significant decline in walking. Lifting, carrying, putting down own children – constant checking of their whereabouts and safety. On feet all day teaching. Follow up desk bound work.	Two family cars – limited walking. Increasingly limited physical demands from children – more the chauffeur. Time in front of computers much increased.
Recreational	Learn to swim, ride a bike. Playing with friends, siblings. Football (and later cricket) becomes an interest, both playing and watching. Organised games – in/out of school contexts. Intermittent PE throughout (games, gymnastics, dance, athletics, swimming).	Football, cricket, swimming with friends. School-based badminton club. Continue to watch professional sport, particularly football and cricket.	Latter part of football playing career. Major period of cricket career. Take up of many different activities – squash, tennis, golf, skiing...job-related. Family ski holidays. Maintenance of watching professional sport.	Indoor football weekly, some swimming, golf. Walking and cycling resurrected. Lots of spectating of professional sport.
Health-related	Walking (and cycling) to and from places. Play and recreation.	Walking and cycling. Paper rounds. Performance-related training.	Performance-related training. Running and limited swimming.	Family swimming. Cycling. Walking.

Perform-ance	School teams – football, cricket, athletics.	Football, cricket and badminton to school representative level.	University – 1st X1 football. Amateur football and cricket.	Limited to personal demonstration of skills pertaining to PE teacher role.
Support	Teaching younger brother football and cricket skills.	Help out with school PE department in sixth form.	Career in PE teaching. Multitude of different classes and extra-curricular clubs. Swimming and general play with own children.	Career in PE but largely deskbound. Taxi driver mode – taking children to a multitude of activities from ballet, to drama, to sports activities.

My personal views and philosophy for the place and importance of primary physical education – ITE student (Year 2 undergraduate)

A baby uses movement in a variety of ways from its very first day, not only to explore its surroundings and to investigate attractive objects within its grasp but to also gain responses from its parents and other adults. Basic actions of rolling, rocking, climbing, running, etc. are often fully explored by the time a child reaches school age (Maude, 2001). However, it is important that children are given the opportunity to develop these skills along with 'coordination, control and manipulation' through physical education/development' (QCA 2000: 100).

It has been said that physical play is not only a prerequisite for physical and emotional development, but is also the most accessible and natural vehicle to use in the promotion of the development of children's intellect (Tanner, 1978). More recent research has shown that sport and physical activity plays a critical role in educating the *whole* child and 'has the potential to improve a child's body and mind and raise the quality of their education' (Johnson, 2002). Gallahue and Donnelly (2003: 10) explain that the basic aim of physical education is simply that there should be a portion of the school day set aside devoted to large muscle activities that encourage and develop *learning to move* and *learning through movement*. If children are given this opportunity I believe along with Paglin (2000) and Gallahue and Donnelly (2003) that they will then have the energy to concentrate and carry out work with enthusiasm. Quality physical education is not only a programme that provides children with opportunities to learn motor skills, develop fitness and gain understanding about physical activity, it can also promote social cooperative ability, self-expression, conflict resolution and problem-solving competencies life skills that all people need (National Association for Sport and Physical Education, 2001). It has also been said that physical education enables children to remember and retain information (Paglin, 2000). In my opinion and quite crucially, physical education has the potential to improve children's health, helping to stave off problems like heart disease, diabetes and obesity (Postnote, 2003). Armstrong (1996) states that physical activity stimulates a sense of well-being, reduces stress and improves self-esteem (in Maude, 2001: 125). Many children are able to achieve significantly in PE where they are not so successful in other subjects.

With the growing world of technology, it is quite obvious that exercise is no longer a regular part of everyone's day. Indeed many children never walk or cycle to school, or play any kind of sport. A rise in inactive activities – such as watching television, playing computer games or accessing the Internet have taken over children's pastimes. For example in 2002 it was recorded that the average 4–5 year old watched 2.5 hours of television a day (Postnote, 2003). These aspects have made immense contributions to the rise in childhood obesity. It has been estimated that 15 per cent of children in the UK are overweight or obese, suggesting that children are simply not burning sufficient calories or using enough energy to remain healthy. With the implementation of *Healthy Eating* and *Healthy Lifestyle* programmes within the school curriculum, schools have now taken on the role of promoting healthy living (DfEE, 1999: 129). Physical education enables children to not only take part in exercise, but also to learn about the links between exercise and health. Children then become able to incorporate physical activity into their everyday routine, for example by walking, using the stairs instead of a lift, and so on. If children are doing this at an early age it will pay huge dividends later in life (Johnson, 2002).

The identification of benefits to be accrued from well taught physical education, and an understanding of what good physical education looks like in primary school provision, will provide you with an opportunity to reflect on where you personally stand with regard to the subject.

To rationalise further the role of the subject in children's education it is worth visiting the question *'What would the school curriculum look like without physical education?'* Clearly the education of 'the whole child' is not possible without the physical side being addressed. This opens up the debate about the subject's purpose, its possible content, the teaching approaches to adopt for different needs and age groups within primary provision, how we might evaluate outcomes, and so forth. As we strive to improve the standards of our teaching of PE, it helps to have a personal philosophy for the teaching of the subject and to be fully aware of the need to revisit and update this as experience accrues over time and as changes impact on educational provision across the board.

PE is above all an *active* subject, where children can visibly *show immediately* their grasp of a skill or movement without (necessarily) having to wait for feedback from their teacher. This affords you the opportunity to display your own interest in the subject's contribution to the overall learning process, by valuing its uniqueness and promoting not just learning for its own sake, but also the extrinsic enjoyment, fun and reward the subject brings to its participants, namely for children and teachers alike. By this is meant that *all participants* can benefit from the experiences and opportunities that the subject offers.

PE in primary schools needs to serve a variety of different purposes. Foremost amongst these should be the importance of teaching children about the need for regular and healthy exercise, the understanding required to identify how important our body is to an active lifestyle, and respect for the fact that with regular exposure to a breadth and variety of physical activity, children can become increasingly skilled, motor competent and self-confident in what their bodies can do. Along the way to achieving this they should also derive fun and enjoyment through participation that is physically orientated, contributes to levels of personal fitness, has social dimensions, and is by and large appealing to the majority of children.

In order to teach PE effectively you ultimately need to be aware of the key role the subject plays in the all-round development of children during the primary phase of learning. Additionally, you require a knowledge base about the subject in order to develop your own confidence in teaching the subject effectively and meeting these needs. This process takes time, and can be nurtured through an appreciation of the subject's worth and its natural appeal to children. If there is also enthusiasm, interest and vitality when confronted with the demands of teaching the subject, then it is highly likely that there will be benefits for everyone engaged in this particular teaching and learning context.

So in developing a personal rationale and philosophy for teaching PE consider Figure 1.1 below and put into your own development practice the following.

- Examine the nature and purpose of the subject and its place in the education of children in the primary phase.
- Develop a broad base of knowledge and skills from which you can classify movement in ways relevant to the physical development learning area of the Foundation Stage, as well as the areas of activity as cited for Key Stage 1 and Key Stage 2 of the National Curriculum.
- Identify and be able to apply the basic principles underlying the teaching of the specific skills and movement competences identified within Foundation Stage and National Curriculum physical development and education.

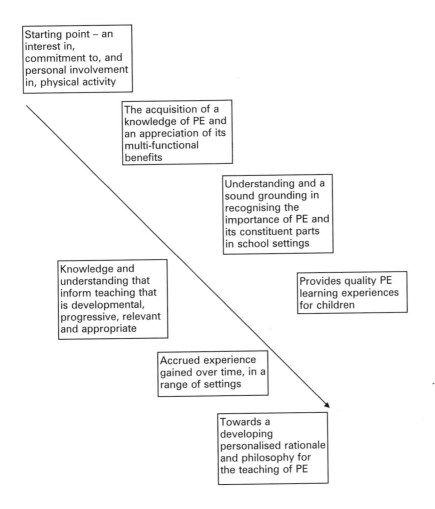

Figure 1.1 Continuum of acquiring a personal rationale and philosophy for teaching primary physical education

To support, help and nurture this, you will need to undertake these tasks.

- Engage in an honest, reflective and analytical assessment of what children currently know, what they understand and what they can do in PE.
- Continue to build your own personal profile of professional development through ongoing CPD.
- Create opportunities to share ideas and pool knowledge with fellow teachers and professionals.
- Work to ensure that the PE undertaken by children is progressively more challenging and demanding – this is best achieved by regular assessment of their planning, performance and evaluation skills.
- Ensure that children have an adequate range of (and opportunity to use) suitable and appropriate materials, equipment and resources when participating in PE activities.
- Consistently push children's learning beyond basic understanding and competence.
- Provide the balance of educational experience within the subject of PE itself and the curriculum generally – recognising in doing so that the subject, beyond its immediate focus on developing locomotor, stability and manipulative competence, also contributes markedly to problem solving and related analytic, language and numeracy skills.

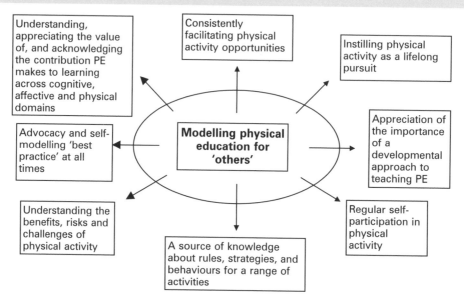

Figure 1.2 Modelling physical education for 'others'

A SUMMARY OF **KEY POINTS**

This chapter has sought to detail why the subject of physical education in primary schools is so important to children's all-round education and development. When pressed to articulate the physical, cognitive and affective domains of learning that the subject contributes to, teachers need to know the benefits that can accrue from learning in the area, both for the children they teach as well as for themselves.

An understanding and ever-developing knowledge base of what quality physical education looks like in practice will help teachers to recognise those key characteristics and features of good practice that contribute to presenting all aspects of the subject in its most positive light. When confronted with the challenge of making a case for securing further resources for the teaching of the subject, or to support personal training needs for yourself or others, it helps greatly to be able to draw from a secure base of knowledge about the subject in support of the particular case you are making.

Furthermore, out of this knowledge and understanding, a personal rationale and philosophy for the subject can be nurtured, developed over time, and influenced by regular engagement with the subject. Knowing why we are teaching a subject, its purpose and function, and above all recognising its contribution to children's all round development, help to ensure that the subject is taken seriously and is taught regularly, consistently and to a high standard with every chance of seeing children gain the maximum benefit as a result.

REFERENCES REFERENCES **REFERENCES** REFERENCES REFERENCES REFERENCES

Armstrong, N. (1996) cited in Maude, P. (2001) *Physical Children, Active Teaching: Investigating Physical Literacy*. Buckingham: Open University.

Bailey, R. (2001) *Teaching Physical Education – A Handbook for Primary & Secondary School Teachers.* London: Kogan Page Ltd.

DfEE (1999) *Physical Education in the National Curriculum*. London: DfEE and the QCA.

Gallahue, D.L. and Donnelly, F.C. (2003) *Developmental Physical Education for All Children*. Champaign, IL: Human Kinetics.

Jess, M. (2004) *Basic Moves*. Edinburgh: The University of Edinburgh.

Johnson, A. (2002) cited in *Teaching Times* (2002) 'The government is planning changes to PE lessons to help children avoid the problems of obesity, Education Secretary Alan Johnson has announced'. Available at http://www.teachingtimes.co.uk/index.php?option=comcontent&task= viw&id=131&1temid=58

Maude, P. (2001) *Physical Children Active Teaching. Investigating Physical Literacy*. Buckingham: Open University.

National Association for Sport and Physical Education (2001) 'Physical Education is critical to a complete education'. Available at http://www.aahperd.org/naspe/pdf_files

QCA (2000) *Curriculum Guidance for the Foundation Stage*. London: QCA.

Tanner, P. (1978) cited in Manners, H.K. and Carroll, M.E. (1995) *A Framework for Physical Education in the Early Years*. Abingdon: Falmer Press.

FURTHER READING FURTHER READING **FURTHER READING** FURTHER READING

DfES (2000) *Curriculum Guidance for the Foundation Stage*. London: DfES and the QCA.

Haywood, K.M. and Getchell, N. (2001) *Life Span Motor Development*. Champaign, IL: Human Kinetics.

Paglin, C. (2000) *Dance like a caterpillar*. Available at http://www.nwrel.org/nwedu/fall_00/cater pillar.html

Pickup, I. and Price, L. (2003) 'The Development of a rationale for teaching primary PE – tracking trainee teachers' perceptions of the subject via use of log/journals'. Conference paper presented at SERA, Perth.

Pickup, I. and Price, J. (2006) 'The Primary Physical Educator – Reflections on the process of becoming a physical education specialist', *Physical Education Matters*, 1 (2) 41-47.

Pickup, I. and Price, L. (2007) *Teaching Physical Education in the Primary School*. London: Continuum.

Pettifor, B. (1999) *Physical Education Methods for Classroom Teachers*. Leeds: Human Kinetics.

Pollard, A. (2002) *Reflective Teaching*. London: Continuum.

Postnote (2003) 'Childhood obesity'. Available at http:www.parliament.uk/post/pn205.pdf

Price, L. and Pickup. I. (2005) 'Different experiences, changing philosophies, challenging times'. Conference paper presented at SERA, Perth.

TDA (2007) *The Revised standards for the Recommendation for Qualified Teacher Status (QTS)*. London: TDA.

2
The content of physical education
Maxine Trace

By the end of this chapter you will have an understanding of:

- the statutory requirements of physical education in both the Early Years Foundation Stage and the primary National Curriculum 5–11;
- how to plan units of work which build upon children's developing movement competence and challenge children's knowledge, skills and understanding across physical, cognitive, social and affective domains;
- ways to make more informed observations of children's performance in a range of basic body actions;
- a range of methods to assess and monitor children's learning and achievement;
- ways to meet the needs of all children through effective teaching and differentiation strategies.

This chapter addresses, and makes a contribution to, the following Professional Standards for QTS:

- **Professional attributes – Q1, Q2, Q3, Q4, Q5, Q6**
- **Professional knowledge and understanding – Q10, Q11, Q12, Q13, Q14, Q15, Q17, Q18, Q19, Q20**
- **Professional skills – Q22, Q23, Q24, Q25, Q26, Q27, Q28, Q29, Q33**

Fundamental movement skills learning: a developmental approach

Through the teaching of physical education, children develop a knowledge of their own body and its movement potential, which ultimately should lead to them becoming more skilful, expressive and controlled in their movements. Effective physical education teaching plays a major role in children's acquisition of 'physical literacy', which has been defined as:

> *The motivation, confidence, physical competence, understanding and knowledge to maintain physical activity at an individually appropriate level, throughout life.*
>
> (Whitehead, 2006)

and

> *the ability to and motivation to capitalize on our movement potential to make a significant contribution to the quality of life.*
>
> (ibid.)

If we look at physical education in this way we cannot help but attribute value to the role primary PE plays in children's early development, the role of the teacher and to the developmental approach we should place at the heart of our PE teaching.

From September 2008, it is mandatory for children aged from birth to five to follow the *Early Years Foundation Stage* (EYFS) (DfES 2007). The curriculum's overarching aim is to help all young children to achieve the Every Child Matters outcomes (see Chapter 4) and focuses on four themes. These distinctive themes complement each other to ensure that the development, learning and care of young children is placed at the heart of all those who work with young children across the spectrum of Early Years education settings. The EYFS brings together the principles, pedagogy and approach of *Birth to Three Matters*, the *National Standards for Under 8s Daycare and Childminding* and the *Curriculum Guidance for the Foundation Stage* to form one all-embracing curriculum.

Section 4.4 of the Learning and Development theme is made up of six areas of learning and due to the holistic approach to teaching and learning adopted in Early Years education, these six areas of learning are never taught in isolation.

The six areas of learning are as follows.

- *Personal, Social and Emotional Development*
- *Communication, Language and Literacy*
- *Problem Solving, Reasoning and Numeracy*
- *Knowledge and Understanding of the World*
- *Physical Development*
- *Creative Development*

Physical Development is made up of the following three aspects: *Movement and Space; Health and Bodily Awareness; Using Equipment and Materials*, and seeks to develop children's confidence, their sense of well-being, their independence, and improve basic skills in movement, manipulation, control and coordination through experimentation and exploration in active and interactive situations. For children to become knowledgeable and skilful movers they need to be immersed in a rich language of movement. From an early age it is important that children hear and learn to use relevant action words and form connections between these and their bodies (Maude, 2001:p51). The EYFS also puts emphasis on children being introduced to movement vocabulary (see Table 2.1) alongside their actions and being provided with frequent opportunities to practise these in 'enabling environments' and within 'positive relationships' in order to become increasingly skilful. As well as this, children are also encouraged to feel and appreciate the benefits of being active and healthy. Teachers are required to plan appropriate, regular and challenging activities in both indoor and outdoor environments, which include a balance of adult-led and child-initiated learning experiences. Children's knowledge, skills, understanding and attitudes are observed, recorded, and monitored, and their progress and achievement measured against a series of early learning goals.

- *Move with confidence, imagination and in safety.*
- *Move with control and coordination.*
- *Travel around, under, over and through balancing and climbing equipment.*
- *Show awareness of space, of themselves and of others.*
- *Recognise the importance of keeping healthy and those things which contribute to this.*
- *Recognise the changes that happen to their bodies when they are active.*
- *Use a range of small and large equipment.*
- *Handle tools, objects, construction and malleable materials safely and with increasing control.*

From: The Early Years Foundation Stage (DfES, 2007). Visit http://www.standards.dfes.gov.uk/eyfs/ for further details and exemplification.

Early Years Foundation Stage and Primary NCPE

Table 2.1 Movement Vocabulary for Early Years and primary physical education

Categories of movement	Body concepts	Relationship awareness	Spatial awareness	Effort awareness
Locomotion **(Travelling)** crawling cruising stepping walking running jogging sprinting striding galloping sliding skipping hopping jumping leaping climbing swinging rolling over **Non-Locomotor Skills** pushing/pulling swinging/swaying rising/falling twisting/turning rocking hanging/supporting curling/stretching **Stability** **(Balance)** static/dynamic posture upright/horizontal/ inverted ready position stopping landing coordination cross laterality spinning body rolling dodging floating gliding **Manipulation** **(Object control)** sending/receiving throwing kicking punting ball rolling static ball striking catching trapping/stopping (feet/ stick) travelling with dribbling (feet, hands, stick) volleying striking lifting/holding/carrying sliding/pushing/pulling grasping/gripping/ squeezing hooking springing tapping/hitting	**Whole body** large parts small parts fixed free near far leading following isolated **Body Parts** hands/feet fingers/toes arms/legs head forehead face eyes nose ears cheeks chin mouth neck shoulders chest knees elbows ankles balls/ heels of feet thighs hips stomach back bottom **Surface** front back side top bottom **Shape** ball round, curled arrow tall, straight... screw twisted, spiky wall wide, broad **Size** big small medium	**Objects/Obstacles** over under beside in between next to to the side of across on to off on top through underneath up down around near to towards away from close to far away from into out of height length width inside outside **People** individual solo partner pairs group team ensemble class work alone work with others copy match mirror shadow complement contrast in unison together/apart in canon alternating cross/pass simultaneously attacker defender support actions counter balance counteract talk and discuss observe describe evaluate notice watch	**Levels** high medium low away from... near the floor near the surface **Directions** forwards backwards diagonally sideways up down pathways (curved, straight, spiral, zigzag) **Space** personal space general space	**Time** speed fast slow medium quickly slowly quicker faster slower slowest fastest quickest accelerate decelerate go and stop sustained sudden short time long time stillness pause before after at same time within set time **Force** strong light powerful firm light soft tension **Weight** heavy light **Flow** free bound

From studying the list above (and further examples of the scope of activities relevant to foundation stage children as exemplified at www.standards.dfes.gov.uk/schemes2/phe/teaching) it is clear that *physical development* in the Early Years is not considered as mere skill learning itself. It is through being physical and moving that children learn about different sensations, their bodies' capabilities, the people around them, how they as individuals can socialise in their environment and what the surrounding world means to them. By presenting learning situations such as structured games and play, children's early learning will stretch beyond not just the physical, but to cognitive, social and affective levels as well. 'Education of the whole child' is a phrase advocated by many who work with children but physical education might justifiably claim to be the only area of learning that can truly achieve this.

Concl.

National Curriculum physical education (NCPE) 5–11

The National Curriculum for physical education has its own rationale which aspires to build on children's earlier experiences. Through its teaching children should be offered opportunities to:

- become skilful and intelligent performers;
- acquire and develop skills, performing with increasing physical competence and confidence, in a range of physical activities and contexts;
- learn how to select and apply skills, tactics and compositional ideas to suit activities that need different approaches and ways of thinking;
- develop their ideas in a creative way;
- set targets for themselves and compete against others, individually and as team members;
- understand what it takes to persevere, succeed and acknowledge others' success;
- respond to a variety of challenges in a range of physical contexts and environments;
- take the initiative, lead activity and focus on improving aspects of their own performance;
- discover their own aptitudes and preferences for different activities;
- make informed decisions about the importance of exercise in their lives;
- develop positive attitudes to participation in physical activity.

(www.standards.dfes.gov.uk/schemes2/phe/teaching)

In National Curriculum physical education (DfEE, 2000) children aged 5–11 are required to make progress in their knowledge, skills and understanding, specifically in the following aspects:

- *acquiring and developing skills;*
- *selecting and applying skills, tactics and compositional ideas;*
- *evaluating and improving performance;*
- *knowledge and understanding of fitness and health.*

At this stage in their education, through this particular curriculum model a child's learning in the physical domain moves into a more subject/activity-based approach. Children are taught the knowledge, skills and understanding features of NCPE through the following activity areas and it is in these that their performances can be ultimately assessed.

- Dance activities.
- Gymnastics activities.
- Games activities.
- Swimming activities and water safety.
- Athletic activities.
- Outdoor and adventurous activities (OAA).

The Programme of Study for National Curriculum Physical Education 5–11 lists the cross-curricular links as detailed in the National Curriculum itself. It should be noted, however, that physical education can bolster children's learning and interest in many other NC subjects and such examples can be viewed in Table 2.2 on page 22.

PRACTICAL TASK PRACTICAL TASK **PRACTICAL TASK** PRACTICAL TASK **PRACTICAL TASK**

- How confident do you feel in your knowledge of the *physical development* strand in the Early Years Foundation Stage, including the series of stepping stones which help to structure children's development towards their achievement in the early learning goals?
- How extensive is your knowledge of the National Curriculum PoS for physical education 5–11?
- How important do you think it is to be aware of what and how children have learnt in and out of the school setting before they come to your class, and what will happen in their development once they leave you?

Consider these questions for ten minutes and brainstorm your thoughts and responses.

- Is your perspective different to those of your colleagues working in the same year group?

Using your notes, identify specific objectives for your own continuing professional development (CPD). Record your objectives in your *Career Entry Development Profile* and/or your *Portfolio of Professional Development for Early Years and Primary Physical Education*. Write down what skills, knowledge, understanding and experience you need in order to achieve your objectives.

Share your objectives with your colleagues and/or school mentor.

As teachers we sometimes overindulge ourselves in the use of 'off-the-shelf' lesson plans, activity ideas and set schemes of work. This can be due to all manner of reasons, and perhaps we may think that these are sufficient to use in our day-to-day planning and teaching of PE. Though such materials can be useful teaching and learning aids when they are used with care and integrated thoughtfully alongside current planning, it is important to highlight the need to modify such material in order to maximise children's learning and to ensure that the activities are relevant for each individual in your class. Effective PE teaching is about providing relevant and developmentally appropriate activities for children which take into account each child's own stage of motor development.

Traditional practice generally dictates that primary school children will be grouped in classes according to chronological age, and into distinct year groups. Some primary schools, depending on their numerical intake, will group children in mixed year group classes. However, within all classrooms, no matter how the children are grouped, there will be children whose birthdays lie almost a year apart and this will impact significantly on your practice. All the children in your class will have a unique physical, emotional and intellectual make-up and although they may be of the same chronological age they will learn skills at

Table 2.2 Physical Education – some contributions the subject can make to children's learning across the curriculum (adapted from Bailey (2001) *Teaching Physical Education*, Abingdon: Routledge.)

Primary Physical Education		
Games activities	Dance activities	Gymnastics activities
Spiritual development: dealing with success and failure **Moral development**: sensitivity to individual differences **Social development**: co-operation, communication **Cultural development**: traditional games **Literacy**: prepositions, adjectives and adverbs to describe movements **Numeracy**: scoring, recording data and information, problem solving **ICT**: recording scores, planning inter/intra competitions **Thinking skills**: tactics and strategy **Health education**: the importance of warming up and cooling down **Geography**: research multicultural games **History**: finding out about the pastimes and games preferred by key figures from British history **MFL**: to keep score in a foreign language **MFL & ICT**: to email schools abroad favourite games played	**Spiritual development**: responses to poetry and religious themes **Moral development**: constructive feedback on compositions **Social development**: sharing ideas in composition and appreciation **Cultural development**: multicultural, folk and traditional dance **Literacy**: responding to poems, stories and rhymes **Numeracy**: patterns, body shapes pathways, counting beats **DT**: designing and making musical instruments/props to accompany dances **ICT**: recording notation, **Thinking skills**: composing a dance in response to a range of stimuli **Geography & Art and Design**: investigate lines and shapes found in landscapes and developing ideas to make prints **Art and design**: use observations and work developed in art as starting points for dance activities	**Spiritual development**: sense of achievement through sequence planning **Moral development**: counter-balances **Social development**: collaboration when working on a pair/group sequence **Cultural development**: cultural themes as stimuli for movement **Literacy**: prepositions, describing movements and others' work **Numeracy**: shape, direction, symmetry/asymmetry **ICT**: use drawing packages to design apparatus layouts and record notations **Thinking skills**: critically evaluating and restructuring sequences and actions **Health education**: importance of strength, stamina and suppleness
Athletic activities	Swimming activities and water safety	Outdoor and adventurous activities
Spiritual development: reflection on personal achievement **Moral development**: accepting authority of scores, discipline of activities **Social development**: planning and improving relay tactics and changeovers **Cultural development**: Olympic ideals of national pride and international co-operation **Literacy**: giving feedback on jumping actions, sports day advertising **Numeracy**: measuring, timing, data handling **ICT**: recording times, distances and heights, creating a class database **Thinking skills**: assessing throwing, running, jumping techniques against set criteria **Health education**: relationship between different events and types of physical fitness	**Spiritual development**: addressing personal fears and insecurities **Moral development**: life-saving, sensitivity towards others **Social development**: personal responsibility through water safety, pool hygiene **Cultural development**: discussing cultural norms of body shape and body covering **Literacy**: writing safety rules for the swimming pool **Numeracy**: timing, counting distance, depth, data-handling **ICT**: data analysis of times **Thinking skills**: coaching partners using teaching points **Health education**: swimming for health **Geography**: to identify why certain places/homes in the world are equipped with swimming pools **History**: to research sites of ancient Roman baths or the role of spa towns in Victorian society	**Spiritual development**: adventure experiences **Moral development**: co-operating in climbing/abseiling, raft/tent building **Social development**: communication games, turn-taking, taking responsibility **Cultural development**: urban and natural environments **Literacy**: reaching agreements in problem-solving tasks, instructional writing **Numeracy**: distance, use of compass, angles, coordinates **Science**: forces, materials **ICT**: planning orienteering courses, taking photographs for course controls **Thinking skills**: co-operative problem-solving tasks **Citizenship**: environmental awareness issues **Geography**: draw and use maps and plans

different rates because their developmental age will vary. A 'one size fits all' (Pickup and Price, 2007) model of physical education teaching alluded to in many ready-made, off-the-shelf resources is therefore not coherent with the underpinning messages in this book.

Developmental PE recognises the child as an integrated being – an 'embodied self', and is about the acquisition of movement skills and a maturation in physical competence based on the unique developmental stage of each individual child. As a developmental physical educator you will need to make informed decisions based on your knowledge of the children in your class. The 'what to teach', 'when to teach' and 'how to teach' are all questions you will need to be able to answer if your lessons are going to be high-quality, individually appropriate, yet challenging for all.

Physical education is concerned with nurturing and developing children's fine and gross motor skills through a broad and balanced range of movement experiences. Through learning and developing a range of physical skills children will have the potential to:

- equip themselves with a 'skills set' so that they may access a variety of physical and sports related activities;
- be able to socialise, play and interact more positively with others;
- have a positive self-concept, develop greater self-esteem, self-confidence and 'wanting' to take part;
- develop a better 'sense of self' and make links between their minds and bodies;
- gain personal satisfaction through being physical;
- enjoy a healthy and active lifestyle.

Fundamental movement skills (as illustrated in Figure 2.1 on page 24) are not learned automatically; they require practice and repetition through fun, varied, challenging and developmentally appropriate activities. You will need to be sensitive to your children's needs and their personal involvement in the tasks you set if they are to develop into 'mature', self-expressive and self-confident movers; people who are skilfully able and motivated to engage in all types of physical activities throughout, potentially, their entire lifetime.

Primary PE advocates a broad and balanced curriculum where skills can be acquired, developed and improved over time. There exist three categories of skill themes each containing a broad base of fundamental skills which, when taught within a developmental and holistic PE programme, will underpin children's engagement in later 'specialised'/sport-related movement skills (exemplified in Figure 2.1) where the application of skills, strategies and tactics becomes increasingly complex.

These skill themes are as follows.

Stability

Stability skills are needed for the body to gain or maintain balance during static or dynamic movements. It should be noted that there are elements of stability skills in all locomotor and manipulative movements and if children are not exposed from an early age to a range of movement activities their development of skills in stability can become affected.

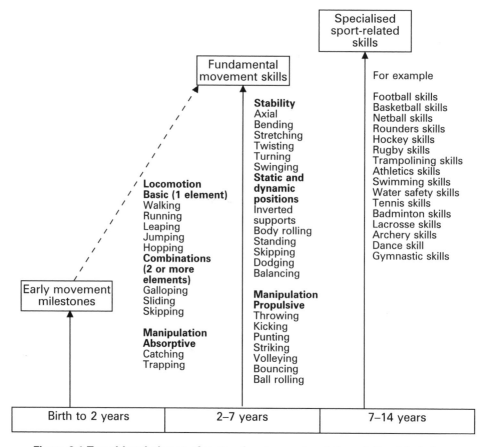

Figure 2.1 Transitional phases of motor development and the relationship between fundamental and specialised movemement skills.
(Adapted from Burton and Miller (1998) and Gallague and Ozmun (2006).)

It is vital that teachers have a firm understanding and knowledge base of:

- the stages of development of skills within these skill themes to aid the observation, analysis, assessment and planning process;
- the ways in which these skills and movements can be broken down into more attainable components, developed and therefore progressed over time.

Locomotion

Locomotor skills are used to transport the body in an approximately horizontal or vertical plane from one place to another. Your children will need to use these whole-body movements to travel through space in the variety of PE activities you set them.

Manipulation

Manipulative skills are gross body movements which the body uses to control objects. In primary PE your children will be required to send, receive and travel with objects in a variety of ways and their skills in object control will be highly dependent on their ability to apply to and receive force from the equipment they use. (In Early Years education, the importance of developing children's fine motor skills competence is also a major focus.

Figure 2.2 The preparation, execution and follow through actions of a child (10 years) throwing overarm.

Children's acquisition of fundamental movement skills will not advance if simply left to chance. In the primary years it is crucial for all children to develop an ability to perform basic skills efficiently and to be able to adapt them to suit a variety of movement activities (Jess et al. 2004). When you plan activities which have a particular focus on a fundamental skill, whether it is *striking* a moving balloon with a hand, *throwing* a ball a long distance to a partner or underarm to a closer target on the floor, *catching* a bean bag in a bucket or *running* to the nearest control in an orienteering activity, are you knowledgeable of the fundamental skills involved and the movement concepts (see Table 2.3 on page 26) which can be modified to encourage children's adaptability and creativity? Rarely do movement tasks in PE occur within the same conditions every time, because the environment and situational factors are forever changing. For example, a child who has worked with one partner for the last two dance activities will find it an altogether different experience when asked to practise and refine the same sequence with a different child because their original partner is absent from school that day. Or alternatively, asking a child to strike a static ball from a tee into a space in the playground and then to repeat the same task inside, in a small hall, will each necessitate different movement patterns.

As a result, we cannot teach one way of striking, or one way to throw, catch or run because there are many ways of doing each and all these skills will seldom be performed in isolation. We can, however, teach fundamental skills through a movement concept approach which is relevant and meaningful so that children can develop an ability to move with control and efficiency, and in creative, adaptable and technically accurate ways. The following tasks are designed to enhance your skills of observation and will require you to reflect on ways to bring about learning through a movement concept approach.

Table 2.3 Movements concepts which develop children's awareness of *where*, *how* and *who* or *what* their body moves with. (Adapted from Jess et al. (2004).)

Space (Where)	Effort (How)	Relationships (Who/What with)
Space self space general space **Directions** forwards backwards sideways diagonal **Pathways** curve straight (direct) curled **Levels** high/medium/low	**Speed** fast/slow gradual/sudden erratic/sustained **Force** heavy/soft light/strong **Flow** smooth/jerky bound/free	**Body parts** identify body shape wide/narrow twisted symmetrical asymmetrical **Objects** over/under/through in/out front/behind on/off **People** co-operative mirror shadow unison/canon competitive chase/flee attack/defend

PRACTICAL TASK PRACTICAL TASK **PRACTICAL TASK** PRACTICAL TASK **PRACTICAL TASK**

Stability skill: Dynamic Balance (stages of development)

Study each of the photographs below and the observation and analysis guidance pertaining to the initial, elementary and mature stages of this skill. Consider what level of proficiency you think each child is showing by comparing what you can see with the stage descriptions. Make a note of your answers.

Following this, write down any additional evidence you would need and/or tasks you would facilitate in order to make more accurate assessments of each of these children's performances. (The observation and analysis guidance here is adapted from Gallahue and Ozmun (2006) p204.)

(a)　　　　　　　　　　(b)　　　　　　　　　　(c)

Figure 2.3 Dynamic balance

Observation and analysis of skill at the **initial** stage	Observation and analysis of skill at the **elementary** stage	Observation and analysis of skill at the **mature** stage
• Balances with support • Walks forward while holding on to a spotter for support • Uses follow-step with dominant foot lead • Eyes focus on feet • Body rigid • No compensating movements	• Uses a follow-step with dominant foot lead • Eyes focus on the beam • May press one arm to trunk while trying to balance with other • Loses balance easily • Limited compensating movements • Can move forward, backward and sideways but requires considerable concentration and effort	• Uses alternate stepping action • Eyes focus beyond beam • Both arms used at will to aid balance • Can move forward, backward, and sideways with assurance and ease • Movements are fluid, relaxed and in control • May lose balance occasionally

PRACTICAL TASK PRACTICAL TASK PRACTICAL TASK PRACTICAL TASK PRACTICAL TASK

Locomotor skill: Climbing (stages of development)

Study the example activities below and decide which you think would help each of the children above to make progress and enhance their performance. Can you think of any alternatives? (The observation and analysis guidance here is adapted from *Observing Children Moving*. PEA UK 2003.)

- Climb up and down stairs touching as many coloured markers as possible.
- Climb up, down and across a climbing wall.
- Crawl on hands and feet along a ladder drawn on the ground—human Snakes and Ladders.
- Climb a steep ladder incline, up and down.
- Instruct a partner to climb up, across and down a climbing frame.
- Crawl on hands and knees along different pathways (marked/unmarked) in the space, collecting various objects along the way.
- Climb up, across, down and through a rope frame.
- Crawl on hands and knees/feet along a line/plank/bench on the floor.

(a) (b) (c)

Figure 2.4 Climbing

Observation and analysis of skill at the **initial** stage	Observation and analysis of skill at the **elementary** stage	Observation and analysis of skill at the **mature** stage
• Body lacks stability • Body leans forward towards the equipment • Body flexes at hips • Eyes focusing on the soft-play cylinder • Leading leg feels for the step • Leading leg pushes down on the soft-play bridge and second leg joins it on the same step • Both hands reach to grasp the soft-play cylinder and join the other • Arms held to pull body up • 'Homologous' stage: uneven rhythm of movements, i.e. first leg, second leg, first arm, second arm	• Body balanced and controlled parallel to ladder • Hips not extended fully • Eyes focusing forward and up • Accurate placement of foot • Smooth, continuous stepping action • Knee extends to push body up • Hand neatly holds and releases each rung • Elbow extends to reach for rung • Elbow flexes to help pull body up • 'Homo-lateral' stage: even rhythm of movements, i.e. first leg and same side hand, then second leg and same side hand	• Body balanced and controlled parallel to ladder • Hip and knee of supporting foot extend • Eyes focusing forward and up • Accurate placement of foot • Smooth, continuous stepping action • Knee extends fully to push body up • Hand neatly holds and releases each rung • Elbow extends to reach for rung • Elbow flexes to help pull body up • 'Cross-lateral' stage: Even rhythm, i.e. left arm and right leg, then right arm and left leg

PRACTICAL TASK PRACTICAL TASK **PRACTICAL TASK** PRACTICAL TASK **PRACTICAL TASK**

Manipulation skill: overarm throwing (stages of development)

Study the three photographs in Figure 2.2 (see p.25) which depict a child throwing overarm. Using the specified headings body and eyes, arms and hands, legs and feet, analyse the throwing action through the preparation, execution and follow-through sequence making a note of your answers.

Next, consider the feedback you would give to the child for each part of the throwing sequence and the key teaching points you would communicate to help this child make progress. (Observational and analysis guidance here is adapted from Gallahue and Ozmun (2006) p 228.)

(a) (b) (c)

Figure 2.5 Overarm throwing

Observation and analysis of skill at the **initial** stage	Observation and analysis of skill at the **elementary** stage	Observation and analysis of skill at the **mature** stage
• Action is mainly from the elbow • Elbow of throwing arm remains in front of the body; action resembles a push • Fingers spread at release • Follow-through is forward and downward • Trunk remains perpendicular to target • Little rotary action during throw • Body weight shifts slightly rearward to maintain balance • Feet remain stationary • Often purposeless shifting of feet during preparation for throw	• In preparation arm is swung upward, sideward and backward to a position of elbow flexion • Ball is held behind head • Arm is swung forward, high over shoulder • Trunk rotates toward throwing side during preparatory action • Shoulders rotate toward throwing side • Trunk flexes forward with forward motion of arm • Definite forward shift of bodyweight • Steps forward with leg on same side as throwing arm	• Arm is swung backward in preparation • Opposite elbow is raised for balance as a preparatory action in the throwing arm • Throwing elbow moves forward horizontally as it extends • Forearm rotates and thumb points downward • Trunk markedly rotates to throwing side during preparatory action • Throwing shoulder drops slightly • Definite rotation through hips, legs, spine, and shoulders during throw • Weight during preparatory movement is on rear foot • As weight is shifted, there is a step with opposite foot

Planning

In the primary school environment we are constantly asking children to consider their actions and ideas carefully and with purpose, whether these are:

- learning to complete the 'first join' in handwriting;
- structuring a scientific investigation;
- responding to a question both orally and in writing;
- drafting a letter protesting to planning proposals for a large superstore to be opened in the local community;
- explaining a clay sculpting technique to a partner.

All facets of planning promote critical thinking and reflection. A good teacher will think through the substance of their long-, medium- and short-term plans to ensure that effective, inclusive and progressive learning and teaching are the results. Planning ahead also minimises potential difficulties and allows for more proactive rather than reactive behaviour when faced with a problem or challenge.

CASE STUDY

It is the summer term and an inner city Year 6 class of 30 children is profiting from the close proximity of the local park; their teacher has made a last minute decision to take them there to play rounders, an activity seemingly enjoyed by all. On arrival the teacher sends the children off to jog to a distant tree and back as a warm-up while she sets up the rounders pitch. Upon their return, the two first children to arrive are instructed to pick their teams for the next hour. As one might predict, there follow various moans and groans from those more-able and competitive children when certain peers are selected to join them. The teacher then decides which team is to field first and this team is left to position themselves on the pitch. More disappointment and arguments ensue. Most of the striking team form a queue behind the 'backstop', in the form of five pupils who are disputing who should bat first. The teacher takes up a position from where she can see the entire class. Ten minutes later the game starts. Some players in the striking team are already playing pat-a-cake with their friends, some have made a daisychain 18 daisies long, while others are eagerly watching the game unfold and waiting for their turn to face the bowling. Certain members of the fielding team are throwing balls to whoever is shouting at them the loudest, some are standing around having a chat to their neighbours about whether not being able to strike a rounders ball entitles you to run, while others are perching on the balls of their feet with hands cupped, optimistically waiting for the miracle shot. Unfortunately, and before everyone has had a fair chance at striking and fielding, the teacher decides she has had enough of the negative and argumentative behaviour and ends the game in order to head back to school.

This example may seem extreme but disappointingly it does still happen.

REFLECTIVE TASK
REFLECTIVE TASK

Make a list of all the poor teaching and learning encounters this PE experience demonstrated and state what the teacher could have done differently. Consider the knowledge, skills and understanding you would expect Year 6 children to have by this time in their primary physical education experience.

The decisions you make about your physical education lessons and the high expectations you have of your children will determine the outcomes of their learning experience. Lesson plans should form part of a wider preparation process and however big the complexities involved in planning for high quality PE are, they still need to be in place. They should also be developed from the aims and objectives set out in the school's long- and medium-term plans for the subject.

Long-term planning or curriculum mapping is usually a task completed by subject leaders and should be dictated by:

- NC requirements; individual schools' policies;
- evidence of what learning has occurred in the Early Years Foundation Stage or previous age phase;
- the skills, knowledge and understanding you would hope for the children to have acquired at the end of the long-term plan.

The importance of a coherent and progressive curriculum and effective curriculum mapping is explored in greater depth in Chapter 4.

Medium-term plans or units of work can be described as a sequence of related learning experiences and are as important (if not more so) than individual lesson plans, as they provide the overall picture of how the learning activities will progress across a period of time. This does not mean, however, that a teacher cannot veer away from this written structure or amend parts of the content. Indeed, a reflective teacher will recognise the need to change and annotate medium-term plans as each lesson unfolds. If reflection and self-evaluation were not features of a teacher's professional practice, lessons would become ineffectual and children's learning and achievement would stagnate.

Individual lesson plans provide immediate and the most up-to-date guidance for teaching and are developed from the medium-term plan. They present information based upon a teacher's latest assessments of children and should be detailed enough for anyone to teach from. Often, the process involved in planning for the short term can be alleviated if the medium-term plan from which it has grown has been prepared with the necessary depth (Bailey, 2001).

To make a decision to fill a lesson space on a timetable dedicated to Physical Education based on a last minute whim can and will never be good practice. Consider the earlier rounders example – could anyone have taught from that lesson plan? Did a lesson plan even exist? If it did not, what does that suggest about the school's medium- and long-term plans? What does it suggest about that teacher's own understanding of the value and importance of physical education? There may be many reasons why lessons such as these still occur, but in today's political climate where the profile and status of physical education is undergoing tremendous augmentation, and where there is great support for teachers through national strategies and the subject's association, lack of planning is inexcusable.

The following templates will provide you with prompts to consider when planning for both the medium and short term and will offer useful planning structures from which to work. Key features of the templates are explored later in this chapter.

Effective planning in physical education is the same as in any other subject. What makes planning for this subject different is the content of lessons and the environment in which you and your children work: '... effective learning requires good teaching regardless of the subject' (Raymond, 1998: 98). Knowing whether you have designed effective learning experiences for children will occur during your engagement in self-reflection and in the post-lesson evaluation process. You will need to take the necessary time to fully reflect on each learning episode that you plan and to make the necessary adjustments to your plans if you are aiming to guarantee your children experiences which build on what they already know and can do.

REFLECTIVE TASK

Study the questions below. How many of them do you already consider before/during/after you have taught a physical education lesson? If you identify any questions which you rarely or never contemplate, how much do you think your lessons would change if you did? How much of an impact on children's learning, achievement and progress would your thoughts on these issues have? Can you add your own questions to those provided below which you regard as pertinent to your personal approach and style?

Learning

- Are the children clear about the main learning intention and how learning is being developed?
- Do I have an in-depth understanding of the topics and am I using appropriate vocabulary?

Organisation

- Am I doing sufficient organisation prior to the activity?
- Am I allowing children enough time to acquire, develop, practise, select and refine their skills?
- How have I planned to use support staff?
- Does my planning show awareness of the human and physical environment in promoting learning?

Introductions

- Do my introductions engage the children?
- Do I make use of the children's experiences and interest as starting points?
- Do I use children's existing knowledge and understanding when presenting new ideas?
- Do I have introductions/warm-up and a sequence of related tasks and activities?
- Are the children clear about the tasks and activities after the introduction/warm-up?

Teaching strategies

- Do I employ a variety of teaching strategies?
- How am I planning to use the children's responses to advance their learning?
- Am I planning for the active involvement of learners throughout the sessions?
- Is there variety in the tasks and activities I plan?
- Do the tasks and activities engage and challenge the children?
- Are the tasks and activities differentiated to meet individual children's learning needs?
- Do I structure sessions to provide opportunities for children to work independently/in pairs/small groups?
- Do my plans show a balance between teacher input/intervention and the children undertaking tasks and activities?
- Are the children encouraged to bring their own ideas into play?
- Do my timings and pace sustain the momentum?
- What will I be doing when the children are engaged in activities?

Assessment

- Are my assessment criteria specific and linked to the learning intention in the plans?
- Do my plans indicate opportunities for observation and assessment?
- Am I able to assess what the children have learnt?
- How am I using my observations and assessment when planning?
- Am I providing opportunities and support for self-assessment?
- Am I planning for systematic feedback for all the children?
- Where am I recording assessment/achievement?

(Taken and adapted from: *The Handbook of Information and Guidance for School Experience* (2007), Roehampton University.)

Assessment

As teachers we are good at managing children.
Are we good at managing learning?

Charles Desforges

Planning, evaluation, self-reflection and assessment will collectively help you to determine children's stages of learning; their current ability levels, the progress they make, and your own teaching effectiveness. You need to have a clear understanding of the different roles of assessment and the various assessment methods that exist so that you can decide on the one which is most suited to particular children, the environment in which you plan for them to work and the nature of the tasks you have set.

Expectations of children's achievement in PE centre on National Curriculum Level Descriptors and Early Years Foundation Stage Early Learning Goals. Teachers are expected to gather evidence of children's achievement and progress over the period of an age phase to measure against these set criteria. This means that there is a need for assessment to be *valid, reliable, practical* and *objective* (Bailey, 2001) if it is going to provide the necessary information that teachers need to make accurate and consistent judgments.

The assessment we use in physical education needs to produce information about children's cognitive, affective, social and physical progress so that we can present an all-round picture of how well children are doing in lessons. Children's experiences within the planning, performing and evaluating cycle and the four aspects of NCPE naturally allow for learning encounters across these domains and the effective teacher will design assessment strategies that help accrue a broad child profile of learning in PE.

Assessment *of* learning (AoL: summative) and assessment *for* learning (AfL: formative) are only two of the main types of assessment but are closely interlinked. Summative assessment is used to provide a snapshot of a child's achievement at a particular time, perhaps at the end of a unit's work, (or at the end of a term, year, the age-phase), and identifies the standard of attainment achieved by that individual. Formative assessment directly influences what you teach on a day-to-day basis. It is ongoing, therefore informing the next stage in your planning and providing the individual pieces needed to build a bigger snapshot. Whether assessment is labelled as summative, formative, formal, informal, criteria referenced, product or process, all these forms need to help children become more knowledgeable, effective, efficient and fluent in a range of physical activities.

According to Pickup and Price (2007):

> *Assessment is an essential part of any teaching and learning episode. The process of assessment allows the teacher to study the rate and level of children's learning and engages the teacher in analysis, evaluation and appreciation – hallmarks of the 'reflective practitioner'.*

(p 114)

If used during the planning process, the following questions should aid you in broadening the methods of assessment you will use and should help ensure that your chosen strategies match the learning objectives of your lesson, the planned activities through which you are going to assess the children and the children themselves.

Why am I assessing?

- To inform the next stage of my planning and teaching.
- To measure the effectiveness of teaching strategies employed in the lesson.
- To ascertain a wider overview of the capabilities of the children in my class.
- To add to established child profiles.
- To understand how individual children learn.
- To monitor an individual's/group's/class's progress.
- To report children's progress to parents/carers/headteacher/governors.
- To engage in discussion with colleagues and other professionals.
- To offer children feedback and suggestions for improvement.
- To find out if a child is able/unable to do a specific task.
- To work out how best to group children by ability.
- To compare children's progress against a baseline measurement.
- To find out who best works with whom in the class.
- To establish targets for children.

How will I assess?

- Teacher observation and focus feedback.
- Peer observation and focus feedback.
- Third person observation and focus feedback.
- Child self-assessment.
- Children's written/physical/visual responses to questioning or a set task.
- Children's explanations or descriptions.
- Children's responses to a task card, a videoed performance or verbal instructions.
- Children's responses to tasks which include identified performance criteria.

When planning lessons and deciding on assessment strategies, you should identify where the opportunities for assessment will be. This will enable you to pick those moments in a lesson when you can focus your attention on gathering evidence of children's learning. On very few occasions in a PE lesson will it be possible to make assessments of all the children present at the same time. The very nature of this subject requires children to be actively engaged and moving and the focus of an observation or the time in which to respond to children's performances can be immediate and requires commentary on visual recall of what has just happened. This necessitates a need for teachers to think carefully about whom they are going to assess during the lesson and when and where they are going to do it.

CASE STUDY

A Year 6 teacher planned a unit of work themed *Invasion Games Activities* and decided to focus on improving children's skills in, and understanding of, self- and peer-assessment. The children had prior experience of assessing their own performances, however their explanations and descriptions lacked the use and understanding of specific movement vocabulary and terminology appropriate to the subject content. Their previous self-assessments also presented the teacher with unreliable judgments. As a result, the teacher planned a series of lessons where children could make more accurate descriptions of self-performance and improve their understanding of the role that they can play in their own and others' learning experiences and the importance of this.

Throughout the lessons children worked in pairs and small groups and were presented with tasks in which they had to assess themselves and each other against a series of specific criteria related to skill performance and NCPE level descriptors. This information was displayed in the space along with key movement vocabulary and visual examples to aid children's accuracy. The children were provided with a writing frame in which to record their self-assessments and the comments given to them by their peers about their performance. By the end of the unit they were more able to identify improvements and areas for development in their own performances and could more readily use specific vocabulary in their written and verbal descriptions. The children had found a new desire to engage in self-reflection and they enjoyed being given the responsibility of measuring their own success and achievement.

Helping children develop the capacity to self-assess is one of the ten principles of Assessment for Learning (2002) set out by the Assessment Reform Group (ARG). Further details can be found on the website at http://www.qca.org.uk/qca_4336

REFLECTIVE TASK

A child in your class has just performed a gymnastic sequence with reasonable confidence and some elements of performance. The components of his planned sequence included an upright asymmetrical balance, followed by two star jumps and a side roll, ending in a low-level stretched balance. The balances were fairly wobbly and the jumps lacked height. The side roll was smooth and showed good body tension.

- What assessment strategies would you use to help this child make progress?
- What feedback opportunities would you offer to help the child become a better learner as well as a better performer?
- How do your answers to the above fit within the Assessment for Learning model?

Recording progress and achievement

The approaches you employ to record your children's progress and achievement in physical education need to be manageable, simple, yet informative. They will also need to serve different purposes, as will be discussed later, and should focus on children's learning and attainment in relation to the Early Years Foundation Stage Early Learning Goals or to the National Curriculum for Physical Education.

Your written records could take the shape of individual records, group records, class records and tracking charts. You might include:

- samples of children's work;
- related written tasks that you set for classroom and/or homework use and have marked;
- outcomes of children's work in relation to the QCA Core Tasks (2000);
- displays of their work;
- video footage;
- annotations of photographs or of lesson plans.

The evidence you collect should assist you in making accurate judgments about all the children in your class, their level of understanding, performance and knowledge in PE and across the other learning areas and subjects with which it links. Your analysis of your records will inform the next stage in your planning process to ensure that the activities you are planning match individual children's needs, interests and capabilities.

Your 'individual records' will need to include *an overview of each child's progress*. This could be presented in a child 'PE portfolio', where you can collate all necessary and relevant information on that child's stages of learning and achievement in the subject across selected points of the year. This record can then be passed on to each of the child's classteachers as they progress through the school, so that by the end of the Foundation Stage or the primary age phase the transition to Key Stage 1 or to secondary school (and the potential barriers to progression that are often associated with such events) can be effectively managed. The following list presents the possible content to include in a child's portfolio.

- Observations and assessments of each child's work in PE (made by the teacher, LSA, TA, AOTT or the pupil) which focus and link to *planned, appropriate and progressive* learning intentions, and are relevant to the school's PE policy (see Figure 2.6 on page 37 which provides an 'Individual Observation Template').
- A tracker of each child's progress spanning all four aspects of NCPE across the six activity areas.
- A record of the teaching and learning styles and strategies most appropriate to that child's needs.
- Details relating to the on-going and future planning of activities specific for that child's needs.
- Records of conversations you might have had with children, or that children have had with each other.
- Video footage and/or still images which allow for the portrayal and reflection of a child's work in and after lessons.
- Children's own diaries and their own written commentaries.
- Details of where the child currently sits within NC attainment levels.
- Information regarding the child's social, cognitive, physical and affective development.
- Information about the child's ability to transfer skill knowledge across activity areas.

Group records allow teachers to observe individuals and specific aspects of their learning against a lesson's objectives. This method will also enable you to keep a closer eye on how your children interact socially when working with others. Figure 2.7 on page 38 provides a simple example of a Group Observation Template.

Class records provide teachers with an overview of children's achievement and progress against the learning objectives of a particular unit of work, activity area or skill theme. The document can be completed, through the use of a notation system, to show each child's understanding during and after the teaching episode. The notations can be accompanied by a comment where perhaps each child is graded on effort as well overall achievement. Once filled in, the sheet will highlight any patterns in children's achievement and aid the teacher in his/her identification of those children or groups of children whom s/he wishes to focus on in subsequent lesson observations. An example of a Class Record Proforma is illustrated in Figure 2.8 on page 39.

Tracking sheets are similar in the sense that they provide an overview, although this method is really a record of the teacher's own record-keeping; it allows the teacher to monitor the observations made of children in different subject areas. Figure 2.9 on page 40 features a system to track whether observations of children across all six NCPE activity areas and in each of the four aspects have been covered. You could adapt this template to accommodate the record-keeping systems in your school and to reflect your observations made across all subject areas. You might also wish to consider keeping a record of whether you have recorded dates of observations and assessments to make sure all children have been

Child's name	Year group and class	Date of observation	Time of observation

Context for the activity being observed and pupil's prior experience, knowledge, skills and understanding (including lesson plan reference/NC reference/reference to pupil's IEP if appropriate):

Learning Objectives (LO) for this child:
-
-
-

Describe: make details about what you see the child doing, saying or how they behave	**Interpret**: consider what this observation tells you about this child	**Action**: after analysing what you observed and your interpretations, note what you are going to do to ensure that this child develops, improves performance and learning
LO.1	Insert symbol:	Suggestions for the next lesson:
LO. 2		
LO. 3		
Comments:		

Symbols used to denote:

Learning Objective fully met ✓
Learning Objective partly met –
Learning Objective not met ✗

Figure 2.6 Individual Observation Template

Date of observation	Year Group and class	Time of observation

Context for the activity being observed and pupils' prior experience, knowledge, skills and understanding (including lesson plan reference/NC reference/reference to pupils' IEPs if appropriate):

Learning Objectives (LO) for this group:
-
-
-

Name of child	LO1	LO2	LO3	Thinking skills demonstrated (information processing, reasoning, enquiry, creative thinking, evaluation):

Comments:

Symbols used to denote:

Learning Objective fully met   ✓
Learning Objective partly met   –
Learning Objective not met   ✗

Suggestions for the next lesson:

Figure 2.7 Group Observation Template

Symbols used to denote: In depth understanding ✓ Sound understanding − Limited understanding ✗	Title of Unit/Skill Theme/Activity Area																			
	NCPE Reference:																			
	Learning Objectives (L.O.):																			
Name of pupil	L.O.1	L.O.2	L.O.3	L.O.4	L.O.1	L.O.2	L.O.3	L.O.4	L.O.1	L.O.2	L.O.3	L.O.4	L.O.1	L.O.2	L.O.3	L.O.4	L.O.1	L.O.2	L.O.3	L.O.4

Figure 2.8 Class Record Template

39

Symbols used to denote:	Title of Unit/Skill Theme/Activity Area:
In-depth understanding ✓	NCPE Reference:
Sound understanding –	
Limited understanding ✗	Learning Objectives (L.O):

Name of pupil

LO1 LO2 LO3 LO4

LO1 LO2 LO3 LO4

LO1 LO2 LO3 LO4

LO1 LO2 LO3 LO4

Figure 2.9 Class Tracking Template

assessed in all areas and that you have not left any gaps. An example of what this might look like for one child can be seen below in Figure 2.10.

Name	English	Maths	Science	Foundation	Observation	Reading
Maddie	G 05/02/08 I C 12/11/07 S 19/12/07 D P	G I C S D P	G I C S D P	G Hist 12/11/07 I PE 18/09/07 (A&D and S&A) C S D P Mus 11/03/08	05/02 /08 23/11/07 20/05/08	05/02/08 27/02/08

Key:
G: Group Record   **I**: Individual Record   **C**: Class Record
S: Sample of Work   **D**: Display   **P**: Plan

Figure 2.10 An example of a one pupil's tracking chart
Adapted from *The Handbook of Information and Guidance* for School Experience (2007)
Roehampton University.

Reporting

The record-keeping systems mentioned above all aim to be *useful*, *manageable* (in terms of the teacher's time) and *sustainable*. They each have a different function but together, if used effectively, would present a broad backcloth of information on every individual child in every class. When schools create a record-keeping policy which is sustained and consistently carried out by all the teaching staff concerned – reporting to children, their parents, other class teachers, colleagues in senior management, in secondary schools, in the wider community support or child welfare networks, the governors as well as the Local Authority – it becomes more profitable and worthwhile. It could even save many hours of hard work in the long run.

An inclusive approach to physical education

An inclusive curriculum does not just happen, it needs to be planned for.
(Theodailides, 2003 cited in Hayes, 2003)

The importance of physical education as being a subject through which children can develop holistically, learn about what their bodies can do, and develop their physical literacy and a movement competence which will support them throughout later life is regarded by some to be the foundation on which the subject was built, and should undoubtedly be at the heart of current practice in primary schools. Planning a high-quality PE curriculum, where children are given access to a range of physical activities that are child-centred rather than sports-based and which cater for *all* children, needs careful thought among teachers and is a whole-school responsibility. Schools need to be committed to raising standards in physical educa-tion and all children should experience success and enjoyment.

This section of the chapter seeks to raise your understanding of ways in which you can support children's learning in early years and primary PE. Through a focus on supporting children with English as an Additional Language (EAL) you will carry out tasks and reading to broaden your awareness of support and differentiation strategies for all children, including those with a range of special educational needs (SEN).

Inclusion

The Revised National Curriculum (2002) states three principles for inclusion which are essential if all learners' needs are to be met.

- Setting suitable learning challenges.
- Responding to pupils' diverse learning needs.
- Overcoming potential barriers to learning and assessment for individuals and groups of pupils.

The National Curriculum guidance advises that differentiated tasks and materials should be employed when and where appropriate and that staff should facilitate access to learning by:

- maximising children's use of all available senses and experiences;
- ensuring 'participation' is a dominant factor in all activities;
- assisting children in their own behaviour management for them to understand the importance of taking part in learning and preparing for work;
- helping children to control and cope with their emotions;
- giving teachers, where necessary, the discretion to teach children material from earlier age phases, provided careful thought is given to age-appropriate learning contexts.

Ensuring the access of all learners to the physical education curriculum requires careful consideration when planning, together with an understanding of what barriers to participation they can encounter on a day-to-day basis. The following list highlights some examples of the difficulties which face children with EAL.

- Difficulty understanding the purpose of the activity, the tasks set and the expectations that follow which could result in confusion, maybe even frustration and anger, and perhaps that child not meeting either requirements or their full potential.
- Difficulty having to rely solely/partly on auditory learning, especially when outside and the environment is noisy or when in a swimming pool.
- Difficulty in understanding key communications, tactics and strategies within a game situation or performance.
- Difficulty in starting or showing a slow response to instructions due to having delays in receiving, interpreting and processing information.
- Difficulty communicating and working with others in performance/game situations, sometimes causing that child to prefer working alone or with particular peers.
- Difficulty being accepted by other class members.
- Difficulty having the confidence to speak out, become motivated and willing to participate. (Adapted from *Module PTA/R Tutor Handbook* (2005) – The National PE and School Sport Professional Development Programme (PESSCL)

As already explained in this chapter, a requirement of the Physical Education National Curriculum is for children to develop their knowledge, skills and understanding across a breadth of study within and through four key aspects, these being:

- acquiring and developing skills;
- selecting and applying skills, tactics and compositional ideas;
- evaluating and improving performance;
- knowledge and understanding of fitness and health.

After studying the list above it rapidly becomes apparent how problematic it can be for learners with EAL to access the physical education curriculum, and the extent of the impact this has on the way that the subject is planned for and taught all the way through from Early Years education to the end of upper primary age phase. Solutions and support strategies need to be well established and used consistently across the board so that children can gain in confidence and become successful learners.

Teaching strategies

The following teaching strategies aim to provide you with ideas for how you can plan to support pupils with EAL in lessons to enable them to participate effectively, make progress and achieve.

The use of bilingual *task cards* to scaffold children's learning is an approach that is highly adaptable to many educational contexts and appropriate for every classroom learner. Task cards promote greater independence and interaction among learners and their use with pupils with EAL can heighten the learning experience and allow for greater linguistic development. Having an ability to understand and speak another language, different to the one spoken by the majority in school, should be celebrated and promoted (Cummins, 2001).

Children who have experienced an instructional learning environment wherein their mother tongue is not embraced can find this a barrier to effective communication. They might experience feelings of not belonging or being valued and find it harder to process information and understand the task being set. Using task cards in physical education lessons where instructions are written in both the child's mother tongue and the school language, and even used alongside oral information can help that child to transfer knowledge and skills across both languages and comprehend the learning concepts relevant to the activity.

Visual aids such as posters, children's artwork, photographs, key vocabulary cards with associated pictures, diagrams of apparatus layouts/activity stations, notations of sequences in dance/gymnastics, storybooks, etc. all serve as stimuli for learning and help to engage and sustain children's involvement and interest in an activity. In PE much of children's learning is about perceiving, remembering, organising, thinking, making decisions, processing and problem solving. To be able to 'read' the situation, understand what is being presented and interpret it through outward movement can pose difficulties for many children. Children with EAL will find it especially problematic to have to rely heavily on verbal communication, so visual supports will provide a different way for them to recognise what is being communicated.

Another essential visual teaching aid at teachers' disposal in PE is *demonstration*. 'Modelling' key aspects of performance can be done by the teacher, by the children, and through the use of video footage or software packages such as *Observing Children Moving* (OCM), *Observing and Analysing Learners' Movement* (OALM) or *Teaching Dance for Understanding*. Children can gain a great deal from watching the performances of others. Not only can this encourage success by stimulating a desire within children to 'have a go' and help develop a cooperative learning environment, it also creates a visual image for children to use and compare when planning, performing and evaluating their own work. (For further reading pertaining to the 'what', 'who', 'when' and 'how' of demonstration see Bailey, 2001.)

Non-verbal communication plays an important role in teaching and learning. The ways in which we conduct ourselves as teachers in the space communicates much to children. Generally, children feel increased motivation to learn when they are being taught by an enthusiastic and confident teacher, and can gain in understanding through watching the body language of those surrounding them. Children who experience difficulties in communication will at times rely on others' eye contact, their body language, posture, facial expressions and gestures to make sense of what they have to do. Training ourselves and our children to become good non-verbal communicators is not an easy task but one which holds great value within the teaching and learning environment. (For further reading, see Gallahue and Donelly, 2003: 195.)

PRACTICAL TASK PRACTICAL TASK **PRACTICAL TASK** PRACTICAL TASK **PRACTICAL TASK**

Work with a colleague. Together consider the following examples of teaching strategies and make notes on how these can promote an effective and positive learning environment for pupils with EAL and raise their achievement.

- Employment of Teaching Assistants (TA)/Learning Support Assistants (LSA)/ adults other than teachers (AOTTs) in Physical Education e.g. monitoring and assessing children's learning in a parallel activity.
- Use of 'action songs' e.g. Heads, Shoulders, Knees and Toes.
- Use of a video camera e.g. employed in a lesson to aid children's self-evaluation.
- Use of cross-curricular links e.g. plotting known fielding positions on a grid using coordinates.

Next, decide on which NCPE activity area(s) you would most be inclined to use each strategy in, and why? Do your opinions differ from those of your colleague? Following this, think about whether any of the teaching strategies referred to above have a place outside the 'PE classroom', for example, in other places of learning within the school community i.e. in the playground, at an after-school club, or in the library. Share your ideas with your colleagues in school.

Your children have a right to a high-quality physical education programme and as their teacher you are responsible for identifying potential barriers to their achievement and for breaking down such obstructions to allow them access into every part of the learning experience within this subject. For guidance on how to provide access to learning for children with special educational needs see Andrews (2005). Additionally, for information regarding the P scales assessment system made statutory in September 2007, visit: http://www.qca.org.uk/303.html.

One model of inclusion which might act as a useful structure upon which you can plan effective and supportive lessons for all children is the Inclusion Spectrum published as part of the National PE and Sport Professional Development Programme.

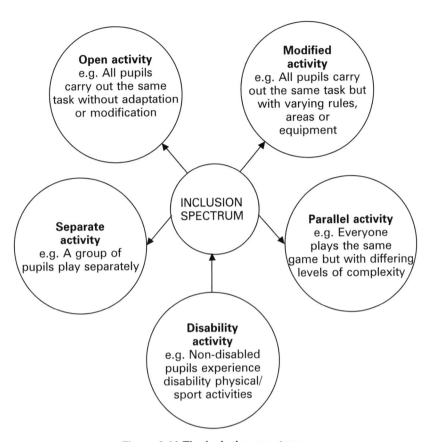

Figure 2.11 The inclusion spectrum

STTEP	Possible changes	Possible variations
Space	How could you change the area where the activity is taking place?	More space could mean more time for participants, and vice versa. Groups/pairs could work closer together or further away.
Time	How could the length of tasks be changed?	Varying time constraints can completely change a task, although less time doesn't always make a task more difficult.
Task	How could you change the actual activity taking place?	Pupils within a class can all be working on different tasks but aiming towards the same learning objectives. Rules and roles are simple to alter to promote inclusion.
Equipment	How could you change what is being used for the task?	Many items of equipment used in PE lessons can be changed in terms of size, shape, texture, material, colour, etc. with varying effects upon the learning taking place.
People	How could you change the groupings taking part in the task?	People can work in groups of varying size and different ability groups. Certain activities may benefit from groupings made in terms of size or role.

Figure 2.12 The STTEP' Framework

The most common framework for differentiation, however, within physical education is the STTEP Framework.

Whilst the STTEP Framework offers very useful prompts, it does not include other discrete modifications such as:

- differences in activity presentation – you might have to present things to different individuals/groups of children in different ways, using different concepts, ideas and language;
- grouping children in ways that allow you to target support and to delegate support staff;
- modifying assessment criteria;
- allowing those children who feel uncomfortable demonstrating the opportunity to explain their ideas to the observer(s) instead;
- practising skills as a whole or broken down into sequential parts;
- when and how to differentiate questioning.

Essentially, the key to effective differentiation is planning and being 'committed to integration' (Bailey, 2001). You might find that your lessons change in style and structure to allow for this more flexible approach and that your children in turn receive a more varied and personalised curriculum.

Teaching and learning styles

How do children learn and is learning in physical education any different?

The 'what' and 'how' of learning are at the core of all learning experiences. High-quality teaching must have a purpose beyond what is assigned in curriculum documents and children's learning must certainly be underpinned by their need to make sense of their environment and the problems that need solving within it. Learning must be personalised.

> *No matter what we specify as the learning objective, the goals of the learner will largely determine what is learned. Hence it is essential that the goals the learner brings to the environment are consistent with our instructional goals.*
>
> (Savery and Duffy, 1995)

There is a long-established notion among educators, philosophers and practitioners of the past and present that children develop holistically through being actively involved in their own learning process (Garguilo, 2004), and that children's direct interaction with the environment in multi-sensory contexts contributes to the reinforcement of language acquisition and understanding. Physical education is no different.

It is not about children queuing for their turn on a piece of apparatus. We should not see children waiting for their turn to strike a ball after a long line of others. We should not see a didactic, 'sports-led' coaching model of instruction at the heart of PE activities. In physical education, as with all National Curriculum subject areas, the teacher needs to act as 'facilitator'. You need to set up activities appropriate to the individual needs of the children you teach, engage their natural curiosity and move their learning forward. Enquiry, experimentation, discovery, collaboration, instruction, direction, guidance, assistance and intervention are not scaffolding techniques solely applicable to the 'classroom' context, but are also teaching and learning strategies that are most pertinent to the PE learning domain.

An effective learning environment in PE needs to be one which draws upon all of these scaffolds and fosters children's holistic development through visual, auditory and kinaesthetic learning levels. All children benefit from learning through these different mediums and their language acquisition, communicative proficiency and motor competence will be bolstered when the learning environment is positive, appropriate, supportive and meaningful to them. The developmental nature of PE should permeate through all aspects of teaching and learning in the subject and the very good teacher will ensure that the environment promotes all aspects of children's potential.

For an in-depth analysis of the whole teaching styles continuum, a thorough read of Mosston and Ashworth's seminal (2002) work would be of benefit. For our purposes, it is more important to consider that there are different styles of teaching and to reflect on why and when they may be most appropriate.

REFLECTIVE TASK

Consider a learning outcome you want your current children to achieve in physical education. Which of the following teaching styles would give the children the most suitable opportunity to learn? Would this be the same for all learning outcomes or even the whole class?

Command style

Teacher demonstrates/models the 'perfect model' of a particular skill or technique for the whole class to copy.

Reciprocal style

Working in pairs, one child performs a skill against set criteria provided by the teacher. Their partner provides feedback against the set criteria. The teacher communicates with the observer to check on progress.

Inclusive style

The teacher sets up a jumping task with two divergent lines of the floor. Performers can decide at which point of the 'river' they should attempt to jump across thus providing an appropriate challenge to their ability.

Guided discovery

The teacher sets questions to be responded to by the learners, gradually moving towards the correct or desired answer or solution. How might you stand to hit the ball? Is it easier to stand side-on or facing forward? Which stance gives you most stability? Does the ball go further if you have a longer or shorter backswing?

Divergent discovery style

Children engage in activities exploring various responses to the same task. How many different ways can you travel on different body parts from the bench to the nesting table without moving in a straight pathway? Show me as many different routes through the cones as you can.

Co-operative learning styles

Children work together on learning activities that are best developed through co-operative rather than competitive and individualistic tasks.

The following list provides some examples of various paired activities which aim to raise pupil achievement and understanding (specifically within the evaluative and improvement strand of NCPE and in gymnastics activities) and meet the five outcomes of co-operative learning (refer to Pickup and Price, 2007: 119).

- Child No. 2 thinks of a series of three actions linked together, and then performs the sequence whilst Child No. 1 matches what they do without any verbal prompting from Child No. 2.
- Child No. 1 thinks of a series of three actions, and links and performs them. Child No. 2 observes them and is asked a question about the sequence at the end e.g. What was the second action performed? Exactly right?
- Child No. 2 starts performing three (different) actions. Child No. 1 gives a running commentary on their performance.
- Child No. 1 teaches three actions to Child No. 2 without demonstrating. (NB: No hands!)
- Both children perform an asymmetric balance at the same time and then compare the shapes they have each used.
- Child No.2 thinks of three actions, links and performs them as a sequence. Child No. 1 observes and then tries to replicate them exactly.
- Child No. 1 performs a balance. Child No. 2 checks for tension in arms/hands, etc.
- Child No. 2 performs a balance. Child No. 1 thinks of one criterion that they will apply and suggests improvements.
- Child No. 2 performs an asymmetric balance. Child No. 1 grades (out of 5) and explains the reasons for the grade they have awarded.

As teachers, it is paramount that we 'connect with' our children and become knowledgeable of their individual characteristics, differences and preferred learning styles. Do you know your children's preferences in learning? Are they visual, auditory or kinaesthetic (VAK) learners, or are some a mixture? The identification, at the earliest and most appropriate point, of your children's preferred learning styles will enhance their learning proficiency and motivate and sustain their interest and involvement in lessons. If scientists now believe that 50 per cent of each child's brain capacity is built in the first five to six years of life (see www.acceleratedlearning.com/preschool/concept.html), the personalised learning curriculum we provide in Early Years and primary settings needs to be high quality and full of multisensory opportunities so that strong foundations are laid for lifelong active and healthy learning.

REFERENCES REFERENCES **REFERENCES** REFERENCES **REFERENCES** REFERENCES

Bailey, R.P. (2001) *Teaching Physical Education A Handbook for Primary and Secondary School Teachers*. London: Kogan Page.

Burton and Miller (1998) *Movement Skill Assessment*, Champaign, IL: Human Kinetics.

Cummins, J. (2001) 'Bilingual children's mother tongue: why is it important for education?' *Sprogforum* 19: 14–21.

Gallahue, D. and Donelly, F. (2003) *Developmental Physical Education for All Children*. Champaign, IL: Human Kinetics.

Gallahue, D. and Ozmun, J. (2006), *Understanding Motor Development: Infant, Children, Adolescent, Adults* (6th edn). New York: McGraw-Hill.

Gargiulo, R. (2004) *Young children with Special Needs*. New York: Thomson Delmar Learning.

Jess, M., Dewar, K. and Fraser, G. (2004) *Basic Moves Developing a Foundation for Lifelong Physical Activity*, The British Journal of teaching physical education, Vol.35 No.2. pp23–27.

Mosston, M. and Ashworth, S. (2002) *Teaching Physical Education* (5th edn), San Francisco, CA: Benjamin Cummings.

Pickup, I. and Price, L. (2007) *Teaching Physical Education in the Primary School: A developmental Approach*. London: Continuum.

Raymond, C. (1998) *Coordinating Physical Education Across the Primary School (Subject Leaders' Handbooks)*. Abingdon: Falmer.

Savery, J.R. and Duffy, T.M. (1995) 'Problem based learning: an institutional model and its constructivist framework', *Educational Technology*, 35: 31–8.

Whitehead, M., with Murdoch, E. (2006) *Physical Literacy and Physical Education Conceptual Mapping*, Physical Education Matters, Vol.1 No.1, pp6–9.

FURTHER READING   FURTHER READING   FURTHER READING   FURTHER READING

Andrews, C. (2005) *Meeting SEN in the Curriculum: PE/Sports*. London: David Fulton.

Bailey, R. P. (2000) 'Planning and Preparation for Effective Teaching', in *Teaching Physical Education 5–11*, R. P. Bailey and T. M. Macfadyen (eds). London: Continuum.

Green, K. (2004) 'Physical Education, lifelong participation and the "couch potato society"', *Physical Education and Sport Pedagogy*, 9 (1): 73–86.

Hayes, S. and Stidder, G. (eds) (2003) *Equity and Inclusion in Physical Education and Sport*. Abingdon: Routledge.

Maude, P. (2001) *Physical Children, Active Teaching*. Buckingham: Open University Press.

3
From Initial Teacher Education to Continuing Professional Development
Jon Spence

By the end of this chapter you will have an understanding of:

- the structure and function of the teaching Standards;
- how the Standards relate to physical education;
- the importance of evidence gathering to demonstrate the achievement of Standards.

This chapter addresses, and makes a contribution to, all the Professional Standards for QTS.

Introduction

Becoming a teacher is not a simple process that begins when you enrol on an Initial Teacher Training (ITT) programme and finishes when you gain Qualified Teacher Status (QTS). A good teacher never finishes their training and will be constantly reviewing, evaluating and updating their practice to meet the changing nature of children and their learning needs.

As someone involved in teaching you will no doubt be reading this chapter with limited time to spare, and keen to find what is of importance to you now – in your current role.

Teaching has changed as a career and the latest TDA Standards will help in part to identify career pathways and the expectations within those pathways, as well as allowing the teacher to identify where to go next in their professional development. This chapter has been planned so that following the introductory paragraphs, all the information is organised along the TDA stages of a teacher's career. You should use this section to aid your development towards QTS and your further career, to plan for your development, to help identify your Continuing Professional Development (CPD) needs, and to help you gather evidence of your achievements.

The Professional Standards cover the following career stages.

- **Q** – Qualified Teacher Status.
- **C** – Core Standards for main scale teachers who have successfully completed their induction.
- **P** – Post-threshold teachers on the upper pay scale.
- **E** – Excellent Teachers.
- **A** – Advanced Skills Teachers (ASTs).

The Standards are divided into three clear sections at all levels of teacher development.

- Professional **Attributes**.
- Professional **Knowledge and Understanding**.
- Professional **Skills**.

The Standards clearly show what is expected at each career stage. Each set of Standards builds on the previous set, so that a teacher being considered for the threshold would need to satisfy the threshold Standards **(P)** and meet the core Standards **(C)**; a teacher aspiring to become an Excellent Teacher would need to satisfy the Standards that are specific to that status **(E)** and meet the preceding Standards **(C and P)**; and a teacher aspiring to become an AST would need to satisfy the Standards that are specific to that status **(A)** as well as meeting the preceding Standards **(C, P and E)**, although they can apply for an AST post before going through the threshold (TDA, 2007).

Each set of Standards can be divided into subsections which are key elements of teaching.

Professional attributes	Knowledge and understanding	Professional skills
Relationships with children and young people	Teaching and learning	Planning
Frameworks	Assessment and monitoring	Teaching
Communicating and working with others	Subject and curriculum	Assessing, monitoring and giving feedback
Personal professional development	Literacy, numeracy and ICT	Reviewing, teaching and learning
	Achievement and diversity	Learning environment
	Health and well-being	Team working and collaboration

It is appreciated that you are no doubt reading this chapter with at least two hats on. Striking a balance between enhancing subject knowledge in one particular area and the general welfare of your class is vital. Indeed, you may have more than two hats on and are a coordinator of a subject area such as physical education, or leading a particular cohort, or contributing to the school's senior management team while still striving to improve the educational experience of your children. Your development as a teacher is essential if you are to provide the children you teach with a positive and productive learning experience.

The balance between class responsibilities and other issues across a teacher's career

					Other issues
					Your class
Student Teacher	Newly Qualified Teacher	Core Teacher	Subject Leader	Management/ Advanced Skills Teacher	

For the trainee teacher a key focus is on teaching and class management, but as the levels of responsibility increase other issues associated with being a teacher, a manager, a budget holder, a subject leader, and so on will begin to take up more and more of your time. It is important to remember that the roles you have beyond your class are essential and ultimately will have a positive impact on the educational experience of every child in your care. Professional development is key to being a good teacher – the work of a teacher never stays still and you have a professional responsibility to reflect and develop your teaching.

From qualifying to teach to achieving Advanced Skills Teacher status

This section identifies and exemplifies some of the Standards at the various stages of teacher development and will help you to understand and develop your practice as well as gather evidence of achieving the Standards. This gathering of evidence is essential as you seek to achieve QTS, pass through the threshold, and gain Excellent and Advanced Teacher status.

As with many aspects of teaching, a key aspect of moving from QTS through the NQT year and beyond (to becoming an Advanced Skills Teacher and into senior management) is organisation. You must develop the knowledge, skills and understanding required and also maintain detailed records and evidence of achieving each standard. You will find the process much easier if you maintain such detailed records of what you do and the impact of your actions on both you as a teacher and on your pupils from the time your training commences.

The Standards

Professional attributes

As a teacher, you have a responsiblility towards the children you teach. There is a good reason for this category of Standards appearing first throughout the range of Standards for teachers no matter what their subject is, especially when you consider the subsections and separate Standards:

STANDARDS

RELATIONSHIPS WITH CHILDREN AND YOUNG PEOPLE: EXPECTATIONS

Qualified Teacher Status (Q1)

Have high expectations of children and young people including a commitment to ensuring that they can achieve their full educational potential and to establishing fair, respectful, trusting, supportive and constructive relationships with them.

Core Teacher (CI)

Have high expectations of children and young people including a commitment to ensuring that they can achieve their full educational potential and to establishing fair, respectful, trusting, supportive and constructive relationships with them.

Within primary PE it is no different. Forget for a moment issues of subject knowledge, skills, rules, health and safety, the pupils and our relationship with them – it is vital to consider how we behave, what we do and how we develop as teachers. As the class teacher we are a role model to generations of children and as such we have a responsibility to act in a manner which has a positive impact on those we teach. Our expectations of children in all areas thus become self-fulfilling prophecies and we therefore need to know what is reasonable for every child. We need to challenge children both mentally and physically in physical education.

REFLECTIVE TASK

- Do you have high (but appropriate) expectations of what children can do in terms of physical movement across the primary age-phase? Do you know what pupils at different ages are capable of achieving?
- Are you committed to enabling them to reach their full physical potential?
- Can you establish equitable opportunities for all children within your teaching? How can you differentiate between what you expect children to achieve and what you expect them to do? Is there a climate of mutual respect, trust and support within your PE lessons? Do you appreciate what all learners have achieved and do you celebrate this?

Clearly, it is essential that a teacher sets high expectations if children are to achieve, and if we expect high levels of achievement and high standards of behaviour these become a self-fulfilling prophecy. Setting appropriate expectations, however, may not be as easy as it first appears. You need to know the potential of each and every child and you also need to set a target which is a challenge but is also achievable.

Arguably, the most important attributes you will bring to your teaching of children within primary physical education are your knowledge and understanding of them as individuals. What have they done? What are they capable of? How can you help them to achieve their physical potential?

STANDARDS

PERSONAL PROFESSIONAL DEVELOPMENT: REFLECTION

Qualified Teacher Status (Q7)

(a) Reflect on and improve their practice, and take responsibility for identifying and meeting their developing professional needs.

(b) Identify priorities for their early professional development in the context of induction.

Core Teacher (C7)

Evaluate their performance and be committed to improving their practice through appropriate professional development.

Excellent Teacher (E2)

Research and evaluate innovative curricular practices and draw on research outcomes and other sources of external evidence to inform their own practices and those of colleagues.

It is widely acknowledged that for teachers to remain effective they need to remain up to date with developments both in their subject and in educational practice. The General Teaching Council (GTC) recognises this, suggesting that CPD is both an entitlement and a responsibility for all (GTC, 2002) and that high quality CPD is essential if the teaching and learning experience is to meet the needs of an ever-changing society. Helsby (1999), Eraut (1996) and others have identified a number of different CPD formats ranging from courses to work-based activities. CPD can be viewed as a mechanism to enable teachers to fulfil their roles but the form CPD takes should be based on your own specific needs.

As a trainee teacher, an NQT or an experienced teacher, you will need to reflect on your practice and identify the focus for your development. During your training you will be required to personalise your learning and to identify your areas for development, and these are reflected in your career entry development plan. These should be continued through a personal development plan which helps you to remain up to date and to develop your knowledge and skills throughout your teaching career. If your training provider utilises a PE-specific profile/development plan you should use this to identify specific PE-related training needs and then share this with the local authority where you teach. As part of the PESSCL Strategy, CPD in PE in England has been funded (and may continue to be) through a local delivery agency which is charged with providing training to improve the quality of teaching in PE.

REFLECTIVE TASK
REFLECTIVE TASK

- List the CPD activities you have attended/undertaken in the last year.
- Remember, CPD can take a variety of different forms, not just attendance at traditional courses. Are these all the CPD activities? Have you observed another teacher? Have you planned a lesson with a colleague, etc?
- How do you know how well you are performing as a teacher? What evidence do you have? Observations? Pupil achievement? Ofsted?
- If you know how you are performing, what are your areas in need of development?
- How are you going to improve your own professional performance? Team teach? Observe a colleague? Attend a course? Read/research?
- What data do you gather in school? How can the data be used to inform practice? How can you use the data to provide colleagues with information to inform and improve whole-school practice?

CASE STUDY

A teacher with two years' experience has worked to improve PE teaching in her school. During her ITT she has gathered evidence of her own personal reflective practice. She has lesson plans and evaluations from her training; she has, termly, written reflections of her pupils' progress in PE; she has undertaken a number of observations of colleagues.

The records/evidence developed during ITT and the NQT have provided good evidence that the NQT and Core Standards have been achieved. In order for her to aspire to achieve the Excellent Teacher Standards she will now need to gather further evidence to show how she will improve her practice based on reflection. In particular she is planning to develop an action research project which involves interviewing pupils and teachers, observing lessons and analysing assessments, as an aid to the development of the curriculum and to identify the training needs of colleagues.

It will be essential that the teacher maintains detailed records of what she does, why she does it and the impact on pupil learning – if she is to achieve the higher level Standards in the future.

What specific actions would you take?
What evidence will you gather?

Having stated earlier that the professional attributes section of the Standards is probably the most important, so too are professional knowledge and understanding. The Attributes

Standards relate to the way we are, whereas the Knowledge and Understanding section relates to *what* we know about teaching and the curriculum and our understanding of *how* we can make the learning experience positive and effective for every child.

You will have covered a range of theories relating to learning and teaching during your training and also as you have developed as a teacher. Learning and teaching strategies which work for you and for your children will change over time and you need to review these on a regular basis. Throughout this book reference is made to approaches which may be adopted in PE and you will need to familiarise yourself with those strategies which are available to you.

REFLECTIVE TASK

- How do children learn and how is this manifested in physical education?
- What teaching styles are most effective (see Chapter 2)?
- How can my/the teaching in my school be improved? What support do I/we need? Who can help?
- Am I/are we aware of developments in PE? The curriculum? Teaching approaches? Learning expectations?
- Are there teaching and learning strategies which you use successfully in the classroom which you can apply to the PE context? What strategies work best in other subjects? Why do they work well? what can you do to utilise these in the PE environment?
- What are the problems in PE lessons which restrict learning and/or lead to off-task behaviour? How have these been overcome in other subjects? Can you apply these to PE lessons?

Teaching PE is not unlike teaching in other subjects. Children need to be set appropriate learning activities which challenge and inspire them. Often a sign that children are not involved in a compelling learning experience is a lack of focus and an increase in off-task behaviour. Providing a high-quality PE experience requires the careful management of learning to ensure success, progression, involvement and the provision of a safe working environment. Other chapters in this book deal with the specifics of teaching the subject, but you need to know the answers. You will develop a range of successful learning episodes in the classroom, so use your expertise to help children learn in and through the physical.

STANDARDS

TEACHING AND LEARNING: MANAGEMENT OF LEARNING

Qualified Teacher Status (Q10)

Have a knowledge and understanding of a range of teaching, learning and behaviour management strategies and know how to use and adapt them, including how to personalise learning and provide opportunities for all learners to achieve their potential.

Core Teacher 1 (C10)

Have a good, up-to-date working knowledge and understanding of a range of teaching, learning and behaviour management strategies and know how to use and adapt them, including how to personalise learning to provide opportunities for all learners to achieve their potential.

Post-Threshold (P2)

Have an extensive knowledge and understanding of how to use and adapt a range of teaching, learning and behaviour management strategies, including how to personalise learning to provide opportunities for all learners to achieve their potential.

Excellent (E3)

Have a critical understanding of the most effective teaching, learning and behaviour manage-ment strategies, including how to select and use approaches that personalise learning to provide opportunities for all learners to achieve their potential.

As you progress as a teacher you will use and witness a plethora of different styles of management and strategies for managing learning. This is a key area for the teacher who is aiming to maximise learning at all times. Traditionally, teachers have tended to revert to a teacher-centred approach and failed to utilise the range of techniques they use in other subjects. PE is like any other subject and you should use your skills to adopt an approach which allows for maximum learning in a safe environment. You should be aware of the individual differences in your class and should appropriately structure the learning environ-ment to allow for personalised learning and the individual needs of the children.

REFLECTIVE TASK

- Do you feel your pupils are achieving their full potential? Is this generally? In PE? In each of the activity areas?
- If the children are all achieving their potential why this is the case? If not, why not?
- Do children experience a range of different teaching approaches in your lessons? Across the school?
- Describe the behaviour of children in your school. In your classroom lessons. In your physical education lessons.
- What behavioural management policies/strategies work best in your school?

You will need to build the confidence to allow pupils to learn in PE in ways that are similar to those adopted in the classroom. You must allow children to progress their learning at an appropriate rate and give them opportunities to learn through discovery. Allowing children to discover movement and to create solutions to physical problems will enable them to learn more effectively and will encourage them to develop a desire to learn more.

CASE STUDY

A newly-qualified teacher has been through a PGCE year to train as a teacher, during which time he attended 12 hours of training for physical education, covering two hours on children's physical development, three hours on gymnastics, three hours on dance, three hours on games and one hour on the other three activity areas combined.

The teacher identified within his CEDP that he needed to gain further knowledge and experience of the various activity areas and became aware of a particular need for personal development in dance.

During his first year of teaching the teacher observes the subject leader teaching dance and team teaches with her. He also contacts the Partnership Development Manager to identify what other training opportunities are available in physical education. The PDM is able to offer:

- TOPS Dance training – six hour module.
- Support from the SSCO in the planning and delivery of a dance unit of work.
- Access to generic units of work within the partnership.
- NQT training sessions within the school sport partnership (with supply cover).
- Access to further training sessions through the Association for Physical Education (AfPE).

Many of the activities outlined in the case study take advantage of the free training available as a result of the CPD strand of the PESSCL strategy in England. There are also other opportunities available which you should investigate in your own context; for example, the Scottish Executive have provided funding for primary school teachers to work at Master's level on subject leadership in PE and PESS Wales has a CPD programme designed to raise standards of teaching in the subject.

STANDARDS

SUBJECT AND CURRICULUM: KNOWLEDGE

Qualified Teacher Status (Q14)

Know and understand the relevant statutory and non-statutory curricula and frameworks, including those provided through the National Strategies, for their subjects/curriculum areas, and other relevant initiatives applicable to the age and ability range for which they are trained.

Core Teacher 1 (C15)

Have a secure knowledge and understanding of their subjects/curriculum areas and related pedagogy including the contribution that their subjects/curriculum areas can make to cross-curricular learning and recent relevant developments.

Post Threshold (P5)

Have a more developed knowledge and understanding of their subjects/curriculum areas and related pedagogy including how learning progresses within them.

Excellent (E5)

Have an extensive and deep knowledge and understanding of their subjects/curriculum areas and related pedagogy gained, for example, through involvement in the wider professional networks associated with their subjects/curriculum areas.

From your first introduction to teaching you will have recognised the range and depth of what you are required to teach and the multiple policies and strategies you need to be aware of in your work. You will have spent differing amounts of time during your training looking at the curriculum for all of the subjects you are required to teach. Unless you followed a specialist PE programme you are likely to feel that you need more time to develop confidence and competence in all areas of the PE curriculum. You should be aware of what the statutory requirements are, i.e. the activity areas you are required to teach, but do you understand the place each activity has in developing a physically educated child and are you aware how the different activity areas are related and why each is important?

You will find throughout this book references to developmental PE and this should help you to understand that PE, especially in primary schools, is about giving children a 'vocabulary of movement' or 'physical literacy'. The building blocks of movement will give children the confidence to move in a range of different situations and environments and the ability to apply their physical knowledge to new situations and activities. The concept of PE developing movement which can suit different situations should provide you with an understanding of how the statutory elements of the PE curriculum combine to produce a physically educated child rather than one who is educated in a particular sport or activity.

As you develop as a teacher you will move beyond the statutory curricular framework and national strategies and will begin to embed other strategies and policies into their work, assisting colleagues to develop their knowledge of these and also contributing to local and national debates surrounding these. This book identifies some of the recent developments in PE, especially those related to the PESSCL strategy and the range of different policies resulting from this government initiative. You will find as you read the chapter relating to current issues in PE that the government focus on PE, sport and health has led to a number of developments which will impact on your work in PE.

REFLECTIVE TASK

- What do you know about the current initiatives which impact on your work as a teacher?
- Consider the statutory strategies/policies/initiatives relating to primary teaching in general. How do these impact on teaching PE?
- Consider PE-specific strategies/policies/initiatives. If your ITT provider utilises a PE portfolio they may have provided you with information about the policies impacting on PE and may have required you to record details about them.
- You may find it useful to keep a log/journal which identifies each policy/strategy/initiative and outlines a brief synopsis of how it impacts on you and the school.
- You and your colleagues should ensure that all of these policy/strategy/initiative documents are freely available in school. You could develop a 'library' in the staffroom to enable easy access to the information.

Remaining up to date with developments in teaching and the requirements demanded of you is not easy, but it can be made easier by joining the subject association (see the Association for Physical Education at http://www.afpe.org.uk/) and using online sources, many of which are free and provide regular updates of developments (e.g., QCA, TDA, DCSF). Using these regular updates will ensure you are kept informed of new policies and initiatives and will also allow you to access national resources and training, of which you may otherwise not be aware.

STANDARDS

SUBJECT AND CURRICULUM: HEALTH AND WELL-BEING

Qualified Teacher Status (Q21)

(a) Be aware of current legal requirements, national policies and guidance on the safeguarding and promotion of the well-being of children and young people.

(b) Know how to identify and support children and young people whose progress, development or well-being is affected by changes or difficulties in their personal circumstances, and when to refer them to colleagues for specialist support.

Core Teacher (C23)

Know the local arrangements concerning the safeguarding of children and young people.

Core Teacher (C24)

Know how to identify potential child abuse or neglect and follow safeguarding procedures.

Core Teacher (C25)

Know how to identify and support children and young people whose progress, development or well-being is affected by changes or difficulties in their personal circumstances, and when to refer them to colleagues for specialist support.

Post Threshold (P6)

Have sufficient depth of knowledge and experience to be able to give advice on the development and well-being of children and young people.

The area of child protection is a difficult area for all teachers, especially those new to the profession. The *Every Child Matters* agenda is central and school and local authority policies should reflect this and should be in place to help protect children and teachers. Within PE you will need to ensure that policies follow guidelines on safety and the key resources for this are the BAALPE (2004) *Safe Practice in PE*, and the AfPE members service.

PRACTICAL TASK PRACTICAL TASK **PRACTICAL TASK** PRACTICAL TASK **PRACTICAL TASK**

- Does the school have a detailed and up-to-date child protection policy? Do you know what to do if you have concerns? Are you aware of pupils who are on the At Risk register? Are you aware of the signs you should look out for? Is there someone in your school who can help you be more aware?

- Look at the *Every Child Matters* outcomes and identify where PE can contribute.

- Inspect the hall in which you teach PE. What are the possible dangers when teaching in the space? How can the risks be minimised?

- Check the equipment you use. Is it safe and free from damage?

- Do you carry out risk assessments on the spaces you use for PE? Who is responsible for these?

CASE STUDY

A teacher is concerned that an 8 year old child in her class suddenly appears to have little energy and struggles to remain active in PE for sustained periods of time. The trainee consults with the class teacher who in turn speaks with the head teacher and decides to work with a health professional in providing the pupil's parents with guidance on dietary intake and sleep requirements.

The lessons learnt by the parents had immediate effects on the child's ability to concentrate in the classroom and to work in PE.

As a PE teacher you will need to ensure that you follow all statutory guidelines and the recommendations of those in the field. The section in this book focusing on health and safety will help guide you through such issues and will also help you to develop your practice to ensure the physical and mental well-being of your pupils.

STANDARDS

PLANNING: PROGRESSION

Qualified Teacher Status (Q22)

Plan for progression across the age and ability range for which they are trained, designing effective learning sequences within lessons and across series of lessons and demonstrating secure subject/curriculum knowledge.

Core Teacher 1 (C26)

Plan for progression across the age and ability range they teach, designing effective learning sequences within lessons and across series of lessons informed by secure subject/curriculum knowledge.

Post Threshold (P7)

Be flexible, creative and adept at designing learning sequences within lessons and across lessons that are effective and consistently well-matched to learning objectives and the needs of learners, and which integrate recent developments, including those relating to subject/curriculum knowledge.

Excellent (E7)

(a) Take a lead in planning collaboratively with colleagues in order to promote effective practice.

(b) Identify and explore links within and between subjects/curriculum areas in their planning.

Planning is a key aspect of the work of any teacher. As you progress through your teaching career you will find a change in your focus and will move from a position where you are planning for your own work with children to a point where you are responsible for effective planning across your school. Planning issues are dealt with in detail in this book and you should recognise the importance of careful and detailed planning if pupils are to achieve their educational potential and if we are to work as effective teachers. The old adage: *'failing to plan is planning to fail'* is never more apt than when talking about the work of the teacher, be they at the beginning of their career or in senior management. Planning can make the difference between success and failure and should be an aspect of teachers' work which attracts regular attention.

PRACTICAL TASK PRACTICAL TASK PRACTICAL TASK PRACTICAL TASK PRACTICAL TASK

- Outline the planning which you have to undertake within your role. Consider the variety of planning activities you undertake and how the different activities are linked. You may find it easiest to divide your activities into categories: long-, medium- and short-term.

- Having identified the nature of your different planning tasks, consider for each whether there are templates which can be used for you/others which will aid the process.

- Talk to colleagues about their planning, and whether there are aspects of their planning which impact on your work or which will help you to plan more effectively.

The format and structure of your plans, be they long-, medium- or short-term, will depend on many factors, not least the systems adopted by your school. You will, as you become more experienced, make the decision to adapt systems and you should contribute to the practice in your school through discussion and debate with fellow professionals to ensure that all planning in your school is integrated and that it contributes to improving the learning experience for all children.

CASE STUDY

A trainee teacher is finding that he is not completing everything he has planned for in his short-term plans and that he is rushing to complete activities in lessons. On several occasions he has overrun and has even had to miss out the plenary phase of one lesson.

- To help understand planning and to develop more appropriate plans, the trainee first observes his mentor to see how much can be covered in a session and also to identify the levels of abilities in the group.
- The trainee teacher then discusses the lesson content with his mentor to identify what the objectives were and how they were met.
- The trainee now plans a session alongside his mentor focusing on the objectives of the lesson. The mentor advises and assists the planning.
- The mentor and the trainee then team-teach the session with the trainee taking the lead.
- In the lesson debrief, the focus will fall on the appropriateness of the objectives, the learning activities and whether the plan had allowed the trainee to better achieve what he wanted within the time.

This training activity allowed the trainee to better understand the planning process and to identify the key elements required in a short-term plan.

As you develop as a teacher you will find that your planning processes will evolve and that the nature of your planning will change. Beginning teachers will need to plan in much more detail than experienced teachers but this does not mean that experienced teachers will not plan. Both new teachers and those with experience must focus on the objective of a particular lesson. New teachers will need however to pay particular attention to the content and the learning activities required to ensure that their objectives are achieved.

STANDARDS

ASSESSING, MONITORING AND GIVING FEEDBACK

Qualified Teacher Status (Q26)

(a) Make effective use of a range of assessment, monitoring and recording strategies.

(b) Assess the learning needs of those they teach in order to set challenging learning objectives.

Core Teacher (C31)

Make effective use of an appropriate range of observation, assessment, monitoring and recording strategies as a basis for setting challenging learning objectives and monitoring learners' progress and levels of attainment.

Excellent (E10)

Demonstrate excellent ability to assess and evaluate.

Assessment, monitoring and giving feedback together represent one aspect of teachers' work which is essential for many reasons, not least because it's a statutory requirement. Effective assessment, monitoring and reporting reach far beyond the statutory reporting of progress and are key to good teaching. Teachers should use assessment to aid learning as it provides them with an understanding of the levels of understanding achieved by their pupils and thus allows them to set appropriate and challenging learning objectives for each child.

The use of 'assessment for learning' strategies is commonplace across the primary curriculum and soundly reflects models of good practice in teaching.

Assessment for learning, also known as formative assessment, is different from assessment of learning/summative assessment, which involves judging pupils' performance against specific standards. Assessment of learning is about assessment to aid improvement rather than reporting about progress.

Effective assessment for learning involves:

- sharing learning goals with pupils;
- helping pupils to know and recognise the standards they should aim for;
- providing feedback that helps pupils to identify how to improve;
- believing that every pupil can improve in comparison with their previous achievements;
- both the teacher and pupils reviewing and reflecting on pupils' performance and progress;
- pupils learning self-assessment techniques to discover those areas they need to improve on;
- recognising that both motivation and self-esteem, crucial for effective learning and progress, can be increased by effective assessment techniques.

This is no different when teaching PE. Good assessment will involve children being aware of what they are trying to achieve, with the teacher providing feedback about their progress and both the teacher and the child identifying what to improve and how to do this.

REFLECTIVE TASK

- Do you think carefully about your learning objectives and ensure that they are shared with the pupils?
- How do you use assessment for learning in your PE lessons? Do you assess the progress of each pupil and give them detailed feedback about how to improve? Can each pupil tell you what they are trying to achieve and what they need to do to improve?
- Do you use assessment to inform future learning for the pupil? For your planning?

It is important to recognise that assessment is a tool that aids learning and is not just a measure of learning. Effective use of assessment will require careful planning and skilful implementation if it is to be a positive learning instrument rather than just a means to inform others about progress.

CASE STUDY

A teacher recognises that his pupils are not progressing as well in PE as he hoped and expected. He consults with an experienced colleague who suggests that he should be observed teaching with a focus on the use of assessment.

The experienced colleague notes that the pupils lack focus and the teacher provides general rather than specific feedback. In the following PE lesson the teacher plans carefully to identify what he wants the group to achieve/learn and shares this with the group at the beginning of the lesson.

As the lesson continues, the teacher revisits the learning objective regularly and uses continuous feedback to identify what each pupil is doing well and what they need to do to improve. The feedback is based on careful observation of the pupils and links directly to the learning objectives.

After the lesson, the mentor asks if the objectives were met, how the teacher knows and what the focus of the next lesson will be. The teacher has clearly grasped the application of assessment for learning and has progressed pupils' learning through careful assessment of learning and the provision of specific feedback based on the learning.

This case study clearly demonstrates the need for the use of assessment for learning in the PE setting and shows how pupils learn better when they are aware of the intention and when they are given feedback which links to their own individual progress. Teachers need to recognise the importance of the feedback a pupil receives and plan the learning to incorporate this.

STANDARDS

LEARNING ENVIRONMENT

Qualified Teacher Status (Q31)

Establish a clear framework for classroom discipline to manage learners' behaviour constructively and promote their self-control and independence.

Core Teacher (C39)

Promote learners' self-control, independence and cooperation through developing their social, emotional and behavioural skills.

For the trainee teacher a key concern is the development of both a positive learning environment and of a positive behavioural management system for their class. The biggest worry for all beginning teachers is whether a class will behave appropriately and whether they can control a class of young children. You will have observed and applied a number of different behavioural management strategies which are available to the teacher and will hopefully have recognised the benefits of positive behavioural management.

Key to developing a positive behavioural management climate is the development of a shared understanding of what constitutes 'good' behaviour. In the PE setting it is important to ensure that pupils are aware of the health and safety implications of what they are doing and that they develop social responsibility within the framework of expectations. In other words, the four Rs of **R**esponsibilities, **R**ights, **R**outines and **R**ules form the basis for creating a positive attitude to learning in the physical education lesson.

The rules and routines you develop in the classroom and that in turn are utilised across the school will be relevant to the PE setting and you should ensure that you consistently apply your positive behavioural management strategies in all lessons, with PE being no different. The development of a shared model of behavioural expectations will then further enable pupils to learn to work together in a constructive and independent manner which will enable pupils to extend their learning within a safe and productive framework.

REFLECTIVE TASK

- Would you describe your pupils as controlled, independent and cooperative in your PE lessons?
- Have your pupils developed social, emotional and behavioural skills?
- Do your PE lessons have a positive learning environment where pupils learn effectively?
- Do the rules and routines you have in place in your PE lessons reflect a framework of cooperation and respect for others which foster a desire to learn?
- How can you improve the learning environment in your PE lessons? Can you use anything you do in the classroom to improve the learning in PE?

STANDARDS

TEAM WORKING AND COLLABORATION

Qualified Teacher Status (Q32)

Work as a team member and identify opportunities for working with colleagues, sharing the development of effective practice with them.

Core Teacher (C40)

Work as a team member and identify opportunities for working with colleagues, managing their work where appropriate and sharing the development of effective practice with them.

Post Threshold (P9)

Promote collaboration and work effectively as a team member.

Excellent Teacher (E13)

Work closely with leadership teams, taking a leading role in developing, implementing and evaluating policies and practice that contribute to school improvement.

Advanced Teacher (A2)

Be part of or work closely with leadership teams, taking a leadership role in developing, implementing and evaluating policies and practice in their own and other workplaces that contribute to school improvement.

Although it might appear on the face of it that the role of the teacher is independent there is a huge amount of collaborative work which you must foster. As a teacher you will work in a team made up of the entire school staff and year teams. You will have a team of staff and support staff in your classroom and if you are the PE subject leader you will also work with a partnership of schools to provide high quality PE and school sport for pupils in your area. As you develop and gain more responsibility your contributions to the teams will evolve from being a member to being a leader.

PE in your school will be coordinated by the subject leader who may also be a Primary Link Teacher (PLT) within the School Sport Partnership (SSP). You will need to work with the subject leader to ensure that you are providing high-quality PE and school sport for your pupils as well as strategic development of the subject. In your PE lessons you should ensure that you utilise all the members of your team, providing support and specific roles for learning support assistants and working directly with any other adults who contribute to the delivery of the PE curriculum.

REFLECTIVE TASK

- What teams do you work in? What is your role within the teams? How can the teams work more effectively?
- What teams function in your area/school that are linked to the delivery of PE and school sport? Do you belong to a school sport partnership? Who manages the partnership? What support structures are available from the team?
- What other teams/groups exist within your local authority related to PE and sport? How can you get involved? How can you ensure your pupils are benefiting from the various initiatives offered by these groups?

Whether you are the subject leader or not, there are many groups who can contribute to the provision of high-quality PE in your school and in your lessons. You should take advantage of the expertise on offer from experienced colleagues, local authority representatives and subject specialists to help you raise the quality of PE in your school and to ensure that you work collaboratively with the various groups and organisations who contribute to PE and school sport in your area and nationally.

CASE STUDY

A teacher who has recently taken over the coordination of physical education in their school has reviewed the provision and has recognised that the staff in the school lack confidence in the delivery of the subject and that this is impacting on the progress of the pupils, especially in gymnastics.

The teacher identifies some key actions to help the staff to develop their teaching of the subject and to develop a whole-school provision which encompasses the elements of high-quality physical education.

- Training during a staff meeting – what is high-quality PE and how it can be achieved?
- Peer observation of aspects of good practice (identified through subject leader observation).
- Work with the SSP to develop a relevant curriculum.
- Work with learning support assistants to develop their role in PE lessons.
- Negotiation and evaluation of training needs – training provided through the SSP.
- Use of local community coaches to provide after school clubs to build on the areas covered in the PE lessons.

When considering the above case study, it is important to note that there is a large team of staff who deliver PE and that systems and structures need to be in place to support this team in the delivery of the subject. You should be aware of the various roles others have in the delivery of high-quality physical education and school sport and should ensure that all those involved work towards a common goal.

The use of outside agencies, including coaches to deliver after school clubs, should not be an 'add on'. These clubs are extensions of the curriculum and should therefore build on curriculum learning and ensuring this will happen requires careful planning and liaison.

A SUMMARY OF **KEY POINTS**

This chapter has identified how the Standards relate to teachers at different career stages and has given an insight into how some of these may be related to work in physical education. Although not all the Standards have been covered, the tasks and case studies should enable you to interpret each standard and apply them to the PE context. Appendix A at the end of this book exemplifies the QTS Standards from a PE perspective and this in turn will allow teachers at different points on the Standards to understand how these relate to work in PE.

MOVING *ON* > > > > > > MOVING *ON* > > > > > > MOVING *ON*

Whatever your career stage you will benefit greatly from understanding the teacher Standards. From this chapter you will have identified the areas where you will need to develop and you should focus on the specific Standards which are pertinent to your stage of development.

Throughout your teaching career you will progress your work and develop a range of different and new skills. In order to pass through the different stages of Standards you will be required to provide evidence of achieving each Standard and to do this organisation is key. You will find it useful to develop an evidence file divided into the various Standards for the level you are seeking to achieve and maintain detailed records against each Standard. If you are going through QTS or have done so recently you will have experienced this and will recognise that to ease this process an ongoing systematic, evidence-gathering approach is easier than trying to find all the evidence.

It is possible to achieve all the Standards in PE but it is more appropriate to gather evidence from a range of different subjects and sources. You will find it easiest if you identify focus Standards in each subject and use these to exemplify particular Standards. As when working with pupils you will find it easiest if you identify what you are aiming to achieve and then how you will assess whether you have achieved it. If you do this you will find that you can achieve the various Standards and – even more important – you will become a more efficient teacher.

FURTHER READING FURTHER READING FURTHER READING FURTHER READING

Armour, K. and Duncombe, R. (2004) 'Teachers' continuing professional development in primary physical education: lessons from present and past to inform future', *Physical Education and Sport Pedagogy*, 9(1) 3–21.

Armour, K. and Yelling, M. (2004) 'Professional "development" and professional "learning": bridging the gap for experienced physical education teachers', *European Physical Education Review*, 10 (1) 71–93.

Hopper, B. (2005) 'Confronting one's own demons: exploring the needs of non-specialist Initial Teacher Trainees in Physical Education', *British Journal of Teaching Physical Education* 36(1) 6–10.

Pickup, I. (2005) 'Supporting the trainee primary teacher: developing a virtual learning environment for Physical Education', *British Journal of Teaching Physical Education*, 36(4) 21–23.

Pickup, I. and Price. L. (2007) *Teaching Physical Education in the Primary School: A Developmental Approach*. London: Continuum.

4

Contemporary issues and primary physical education
Ian Pickup

By the end of this chapter, you will have an understanding of:

- a range of government policies and how they impact on provision in primary physical education;
- a range of contemporary issues and contextual factors in physical education and how they impact on your own practice;
- the current state and status of primary physical education;
- how policy and contextual factors may result in a change to curriculum content in the future.

This chapter addresses, and makes a contribution to, the following Professional Standards for QTS:

- **Professional attributes – Q1, Q2, Q3, Q5, Q6, Q7, Q8**
- **Professional knowledge and understanding – Q14, Q15, Q18, Q19, Q21**
- **Professional skills – Q22, Q30, Q32, Q33**

Introduction

Earlier chapters of this book have advocated an approach to teaching primary physical education that is developmentally appropriate and cognisant of the wide range of factors impacting on children's motor development. To this end, you should take time to consider the range of contextual factors that impact on learning and teaching in physical education. On a day-to-day basis, these of course equate to considerations for planning, such as the availability of certain facilities or equipment, the time available for teaching the subject and your own knowledge of curriculum requirements. For the beginning teacher, such questions will initially relate to the 'here and now', yet as a reflective practitioner you will also want to consider how your practices fit with the broader social and cultural issues of the day. How else can we aim to ensure that our teaching is high-quality, inclusive and relevant?

The factors that influence day-to-day planning do not do so in a vacuum, somehow divorced from the life world of the child, teacher, school, or family. They are part and parcel of the world in which we all live and are themselves a product of various socio-cultural and historical practices and policies. Education policies and curriculum frameworks evolve through time, requiring teachers to respond and act differently across their career cycles. This chapter highlights a sample of current issues and policy contexts that influence how primary physical education is shaped in practice by those aiming to deliver high-quality learning experiences.

REFLECTIVE TASK

REFLECTIVE TASK

The challenging questions listed below will be addressed in this chapter. Before working through subsequent sections, consider your own views and note any evidence that you have from your practice to support these and the implications for your own teaching in physical education.

- Is childhood harmful to children?
- How has education policy impacted on children?
- What is the status of physical education in our society?
- Does the remodelled workforce in school present a problem or an opportunity for physical education?
- Am I *really* prepared to teach high-quality physical education?
- Can physical education cure the world's ills?
- How can I deliver high-quality and inclusive physical education?
- What will primary physical education look like in the future?

Is childhood harmful to children?

In 2006, a group of prominent child development professionals and academics wrote a letter to the *Daily Telegraph* proclaiming that 'Modern life leads to more depression among children' (*Daily Telegraph* letters page, 12 September 2006). One of the multiple signatories was Sue Palmer, who also wrote the popular book *Toxic Childhood: How The Modern World Is Damaging Our Children And What We Can Do About It* (2006). The viewpoint put forward by Palmer and others is that experiences during modern-day childhood have become everything that children's developing bodies and brains *do not need*. This is not a new idea. Writing in 1998, North American psychologist, James Garbarino suggested that

> children are most vulnerable to the negative influence of an increasingly socially toxic environment, and that unless we do something about it now, the situation for children will only continue to deteriorate.
>
> (Garbarino, 1998: 54)

Commentators such as Garbarino and Palmer point to a broad deterioration in childhood well-being, as well as perceived increases in depression, behavioural difficulties and incidences of self harm and violence, suggesting that the way to 'detoxify' childhood 'lies in a human rights perspective on child development. We need to focus positively on what children need to thrive' (Garbarino, 1998, p.55). Palmer's advice centres on ten aspects of childhood, suggesting that a holistic and considered approach to parenting, education, childcare and health provision is needed.

PRACTICAL TASK PRACTICAL TASK **PRACTICAL TASK** PRACTICAL TASK **PRACTICAL TASK**

The table on page 69 lists the ten aspects of childhood discussed by Sue Palmer in *Toxic Childhood*. For each of the ten aspects, write a statement that describes your perception of that aspect as experienced by a primary school child 30 years ago and a corresponding statement for the present day. Which aspects do you think have seen the biggest change in childhood experiences and which do you think could allow physical education to play a role in redressing?

Aspect of childhood	1970s	Present day
Diet		
Exercise		
Sleep		
Communication		
Family		
Childcare		
Education		
Marketing/peer pressure		
Technology		
Parenting		

It is clear that the world in which we live has changed beyond all recognition in the last 30 years, and despite much societal advancement children appear to have a wide range of potentially damaging influences impacting on their daily lives. Many of these influences (such as availability of multimedia entertainment around the clock) simply didn't exist in the past, while other 'dangers' were not as prominent within the public conscience as they are today. Advocates of the toxic childhood viewpoint have, however, faced some criticism – most commonly they are accused of viewing historic experiences of childhood through rose-tinted spectacles. It is important therefore to investigate experiences of childhood against the backdrop of society and to consider the full range of social, cultural and economic influences at work here.

From a movement perspective, it has been suggested that a lack of opportunities for physical play in childhood is resulting in an increase in the numbers of children with underdeveloped core stability, poor spatial awareness, immature fundamental movement skills and low levels of coordination (Pickup et al., 2007). Not only do these aspects impact on learning in physical education experiences, they result in young classroom learners being unable to sit upright at a table or to hold a pencil with the sufficient control required for writing (Wainwright, 2006). The link between activity in the physical domain and broader child development has traditionally been embraced in early childhood settings, where the 'culture of childhood' (Bailey et al., 2007) is characterised by a natural physical exuberance, a desire to move and interact with others. The play context also provides opportunities for children to take acceptable risks alongside their peers and to develop independent and collaborative problem-solving strategies.

While learning through play has long been a recognised approach to pedagogy in the Early Years, the use of such principles in formal schooling is perhaps less common. The move from the Early Years Foundation Stage (EYFS) into Key Stage 1 of the National Curriculum represents a significant shift in approach. Many Key Stage 1 teachers try to build on the principles of Early Years education, but the curriculum structure, centred on subjects rather than areas of learning, provides a very different focus for formal learning. In the physical context, the emphasis shifts from 'physical development' to learning within specific activity areas and the shift from spontaneous physical play to more formal learning is not necessarily a smooth one. After all, why should we expect all 5 year olds suddenly, almost overnight, to cope with increased lesson structure and more formal approaches to learning?

Sport, with its adult-relevant rules and regulations, competitive approaches, tactics and coaching, is in its fullest form not the best vehicle for learning amongst young children. Similarly, the nonsensical development of child-size exercise equipment achieves nothing but the treatment of children as mini adults – something that they clearly are not. Primary school PE, however, is well placed to provide both an antidote to the toxicity of childhood and a gateway to the full range of physical activities available across the lifespan. Building on the important role of movement in the lives of children, using play and the seemingly natural desire of young children to move within interactive, collaborative, physical and multi-sensory approaches to learning should lie at the heart of primary physical education (Pickup et al., 2007: 9). Without this fundamental right many children will continue to miss that golden opportunity to learn in and through the physical domain.

Table 4.1 The toxicity of childhood and the potential for PE

A toxic childhood?	The physical education antidote?
No ball games allowed	Show me what you can do
Sit and watch	Move and engage
Adult values	Child-centred practices
Over assessment	Assessment for learning
Listen and learn	Interact and understand
Safety first	Acceptable risk

How has education policy impacted on children?

Tony Blair, as prime minister of the United Kingdom between 1997 and 2007, will be remembered for many things, not least the commitment to 'education, education, education' as publicly stated on his election to office and backed up by a raft of policy documentation across the 'Blair years'. In schools, initiatives began with the creation of National Numeracy and Literacy strategies (thought by some to have led to significantly reduced time for PE in primary schools (Speednet, 2000)) and have since evolved to include a Primary National Strategy (DfES, 2003b), a Children Act (DfES, 2004), a remodelled workforce agreement (ATL et al., 2003), a re-packaged National Curriculum for 11–14 year olds (QCA, 2007) and – significantly for physical education – a national PE, school sport and club links strategy (DfES/DCMS, 2003). This has seen the investment of over £1 billion between 2003 and 2006 to develop an infrastructure whereby a target of 'two hours per week of high-quality PE' could be delivered (see below).

Most recently, a new 'Children's Plan' has been launched by the relatively new Department for Children, Schools and Families (DCSF, 2007). Writing in the introduction of this plan, Ed Balls, the current Schools Secretary, says:

> Our aim is to make this the best place in the world for our children and young people to grow up. This is why we created the new Department for Children, Schools and Families six months ago, and why we announced that we would draw up this first ever Children's Plan, to put the needs of families, children and young people at the centre of everything we do.

(DFCS, 2007: 1)

Central to the plan is an intention to build on interdisciplinary ways of working, whereby education, health and social services professionals contribute to the development of children and young people through a commitment to the five aims of the *Every Child Matters* agenda (DfES, 2004). There are five aims for all children.

1. Be healthy.
2. Stay safe.
3. Enjoy and achieve.
4. Make a positive contribution.
5. Achieve economic well-being.

The Children's Plan sets out ten more specific goals to achieve by 2020, which are as follows.

- Enhance children and young people's well-being, particularly at key transition points in their lives.
- Every child ready for success in school, with at least 90 per cent developing well across all areas of the Early Years Foundation Stage Profile by age 5.
- Every child ready for secondary school, with at least 90 per cent achieving at or above the expected level in both English and mathematics by age 11.
- Every young person with the skills for adult life and further study, with at least 90 per cent achieving the equivalent of five higher level GCSEs by age 19, and at least 70 per cent achieving the equivalent of two A levels by age 19.
- Parents satisfied with the information and support they receive.
- All young people participating in positive activities to develop personal and social skills, promote well-being and reduce behaviour that puts them at risk.
- Employers satisfied with young people's readiness for work.
- Child health improved, with the proportion of obese and overweight children reduced to 2000 levels.
- Child poverty halved by 2010 and eradicated by 2020.
- Significantly reduce by 2020 the number of young offenders receiving a conviction, reprimand, or final warning for a recordable offence for the first time, with a goal to be set in the Youth Crime Action Plan.
  (DFCS, 2007: 19-20)

The time-based measures of accountability are typical of the performance culture that has spread to education in recent years and are a further indication of the accountability that teachers face in their day-to-day practices. Key messages contained within this plan also stress the importance of play and having fun; the government has made a pledge to invest £225m for upgrading 3,500 playgrounds and the creation of supervised adventure play-grounds for use by children aged 8–13, together with a further investment of £160m for positive activities for young people in sport, drama and art. So, on paper at least, there appears little to disagree with – children and play (which equates within the plan to physical and sporting activities) are high on the political agenda. What remains to be seen is whether the rhetoric is matched by action and practical changes on the ground.

PRACTICAL TASK PRACTICAL TASK **PRACTICAL TASK** PRACTICAL TASK **PRACTICAL TASK**

Work through the ten aims of the Children's Plan listed above. Consider the role of primary physical education in contributing to the achievement of these aims. Are some aims more easily matched with PE than others? Discuss with a colleague the specific actions that you can complete to ensure that your role as a primary physical educator can contribute towards these aims.

What is the status of physical education in our society?

Sport pervades everyday life in the twenty-first century as never before. Newspapers, websites, digital television channels and radio shows ensure that the sporting headlines of the day are never far from our eyes and ears. Our superstars are rewarded handsomely for their activities and are adored by many millions of supporters, while government ministers clamour to be associated with success. Politicians around the world are also keen to acknowledge the importance of sport and – not least in the UK – have been quick to demonstrate a commitment to 'sports fans' through investment and policy rhetoric.

Excitement is currently mounting in anticipation of the 2012 London Olympic and Paralympic Games, the biggest sporting event ever to be staged in England. While the escalating budget and the 'politics' of organising such a mega-event are making the headlines today, the potential for good news stories, the generation of a feel-good factor and the positive engagement of the population in healthy and active lifestyles and cultural activities is enormous. The original bid, led by Lord Coe, celebrated the potential legacy of bringing the games to London and hinted at the positive motivational and educative benefits that would be felt by children and young people across the world.

With the status and cultural capital of sport seemingly at an all-time high, we should take time here to reflect on what this means for physical education in primary schools. Various measures could be used to assess its status in individual schools. The criteria below can be readily used by teachers and could provide an initial impression of the status of physical education.

- Time given to physical education within the curriculum.
- Breadth of activities on offer through extra-curricular provision.
- Amount of in-service training available to teachers and other staff.
- The role, status, seniority, pay and conditions of the subject leader.
- Annual budget allocation to physical education relative to other subjects.
- Qualifications of those delivering the curriculum.
- Prioritisation of practical spaces for physical education.
- Celebration of physical education and school sport within assemblies.
- Amount and quality of planning for physical education.
- Amount and quality of assessment and reporting for physical education.

REFLECTIVE TASK

The conversation outlined below took place during a training workshop for primary school ITT class mentors:

Course tutor: Tell me about the status of physical education in your schools.

Mentor 1: Well, it's pretty high up really; we win the borough sports festival most years.

Mentor 2: Yes, and we make a big thing about our sports teams during assemblies.

Course leader: But what about curriculum physical education?

Mentor 1: What do you mean?

Course leader: Well, you've told me about extra curricular sport. I'm not saying that this isn't important – it is... but what about the amount of PE lessons per week?

Mentor 2: Oh, well, normally two, although I have to admit that one sometimes gets cancelled – you know, it's wet or the hall is in use...

Course leader: OK, so what about planning and assessment. How well is this done in PE?

Mentor 1: (raised eyebrows) Well, we don't have much time for this, but we do write a report at the end of each term.

Course leader: But how do you know what to plan and how to teach if you don't really assess during each lesson?

Mentor 2: Well, you know which children are the most able because they are in the school teams...

Consider this discussion and reflect on the issues it raises concerning subject status and the perception among the teachers that physical education is synonymous with sport. Discuss the issues raised with a colleague in your own setting and consider the implications for your teaching.

Across the world, sport and PE are generally seen as being part of the same process, one that also includes physical activity and physical recreation. In recent years, however, a number of educationalists have articulated concerns regarding what they see as conflicting aims at a time when sport in schools has been the recipient of major investment. For example, Will Kay has argued that PE may, in the very near future, cease to exist and asserts that the very nature of sport is to exclude and eliminate the many until an elite is found (Kay, 2003). If this is the case, then any attempt to ensure that opportunities in physical education are fully inclusive would prove futile and an approach to the subject that was solely based on talent identification and fitness development would dominate.

This viewpoint would suggest that recent policy and infrastructure development in the UK have centred on sport rather than physical education. In secondary schools, we have seen the introduction of specialist *sports* colleges. Schools employ school *sports* coordinators, competition managers, directors of *sport* and school *sport* partnership development managers – a little perplexing when sport per se is not a national curriculum subject. However, the significant investment in PE and school sport through the PESSCL strategy (DfES/DCMS, 2003) has raised the profile of both in schools beyond all recognition.

In a nutshell, the PESSCL strategy is aiming to ensure that by 2008 the percentage of school children who spend a minimum of two hours per week on high-quality physical education and school sport within and beyond the curriculum is at 85 per cent. The strategy has:

- developed specialist sports colleges as focal points for promoting excellence;
- developed school sport partnerships;
- embedded Continuing Professional Development for teachers;
- established leadership and volunteering programmes for young people aged 14–19;
- strengthened links between schools and sports clubs;
- improved provision for gifted and talented children and young people;
- provided a specific focus on raising the quality of swimming teaching in schools;
- led an on-going investigation (by the Qualifications and Curriculum Authority) into the role of physical education and school sport.

The changes in delivery of physical education that have taken place as a consequence of this strategy should not be underplayed and it is perhaps unlikely that the successful lobbying of government for the significant funding would have been possible without a focus on sport as a tangible outcome or dual process of high-quality physical education. In this sense, sport is more readily understood by politicians and civil servants and is perhaps a bigger 'vote-catcher' than PE. You should be aware, however, of the debates that have occurred regarding the structure and pedagogy of physical education, its activity foci and the approaches commonly used.

It is very difficult to be critical of the broad aims of a strategy where a vision of improvement and a guarantee of time allocation and high quality are central. However, several issues consistently arise in on-going academic debate which merit further discussion here.

1. Working definitions of 'high quality' are problematic.
2. Tensions exist between PE and sport itself.
3. Some have suggested that the model is 'top down' and not 'child-centred' and does not entirely meet the needs of all children and young people from an educational perspective.

It is true to say that notions of 'learning through play', so highly prized in early childhood settings, could better inform our educational practices with children beyond the ages of three and four. That apart, it could be argued that any attempts to separate PE from sport or teaching from coaching are somewhat futile in the twenty-first century. In practice, the best teachers are high quality coaches, mentors, leaders, facilitators and carers all rolled up into one. Our focus on policy and practice must shift from debating the merits of different job titles to developing professional workforce efficiency and quality. This does of course not only apply to school contexts, but is equally important in sports clubs at all levels.

The majority of sports coaching in the UK (in terms of hours and the numbers involved) takes place in amateur and voluntary settings, very often delivered by enthusiastic but unqualified or under-qualified parents. If we are to raise the quality of what we offer in all settings, we must also make every effort to ensure that our best teachers, coaches and leaders are afforded opportunities to work with those children and young people who make up our broadest participation base.

REFLECTIVE TASK
REFLECTIVE TASK

The table below represents some perceived distinctions between PE and sport that you should consider. How would your approach to teaching PE at primary level relate to the hypothetical distinctions in the viewpoints below?

Physical Education	Sport
Broad educational benefits.	Skill development and performance.
Inclusive of all abilities.	Exclusive – winning and competition see the most able succeed.
Transferable learning in developmental domains.	Specific learning for performance outcomes.
Taught by qualified teachers.	Delivered by coaches.
Learning *through* physical experiences.	Learning to be more physically skilful and tactically aware.

The notion of physical education as a separate, somehow superior and more educationally worthwhile activity is problematic and a concept that is potentially divisive within the community of practice. It is misleading to suggest that teaching and coaching are two very different processes and that teachers have exclusive rights to the educational benefits of physical learning. Similarly, it is wrong to assume that only sports coaches can facilitate the learning of physical skills and the development of tactical and decision-making awareness of children at the expense of social, cognitive and affective development.

It is more useful, then, to consider carefully the processes at large within the learning episodes planned and delivered by an increasingly diverse range of professionals in the primary school context. The intended learning outcomes, as planned for by the professional in response to children's needs, will surely shape the teaching and learning strategies employed and the approach required in bringing this learning to the fore. Effective teachers may at different times take on the role of coach, mentor, counsellor, facilitator, and leader, and may also employ a range of strategies to both motivate and support learning. Perhaps it matters not whether the lead professional is a qualified teacher or an expert coach: rather, the critical issue at stake is whether or not the quality of learning experience is at the heart of the delivery process and that the strategies used to foster learning are cognisant of the wide range of learning and development needs of the children taking part.

It is therefore pleasing to note an emphasis on the educational value of sport in current coaching policy. The new UK Coaching Framework (Sports Coach UK, 2007) recognises that coaches play a key role in a wide range of social settings. The framework includes the following list of key benefits delivered to children by coaches through sports coaching.

- *Welcome children and adults into sport.*
- *Make sport an enjoyable, positive experience.*
- *Build fundamental skills in participants.*
- *Improve sport-specific skills.*
- *Develop fair play, ethical practice, discipline and respect.*
- *Enhance physical fitness and positive lifestyle.*
- *Guide children, players and athletes through the steps to improved performance.*
- *Integrate participants into sport and their community.*
- *Provide individuals, teams and communities with a sense of identity and self-worth.*
- *Place a high value on the development of the whole person.*
- *Keep children, players and athletes safe in sport.*
- *Integrate the best of coaching and scientific practice into their work.*
- *Provide opportunities for wider social learning.*
- *Promote leadership and decision-making.*

(from Sports Coach UK, 2007: 10)

REFLECTIVE TASK

Work through the list above that relates to sports coaching. Highlight those criteria which are only applicable to the coaching environment and not transferable to a school PE context. Now highlight those which *are* relevant to both curricular PE and out of school hours' learning. What differences can you highlight?

The remodelled workforce and extended schools: a problem or an opportunity for physical education?

A national agreement to raise teaching standards and tackle workload issues has been achieved in England (ATL et al., 2003), leading to new conditions of service for teachers and a series of structured changes to the way that teaching and learning are managed. Central to this process has been the introduction from 2005 of guaranteed planning, preparation and assessment time (PPA) for every teacher, a ring-fenced 10 per cent time allocation aimed at raising standards and improving teachers' work–life balance.

The principle of guaranteeing all teachers dedicated time within the school day for planning and assessment is a sound one, but as a policy has created a problem regarding the delivery of PE in curriculum time. A proportion of the traditional workforce (i.e. the class teacher) has apparently grown a little weary of teaching every subject and some researchers have argued that many primary teachers have for a long time been lacking in motivation, confidence and subject knowledge in physical education. In some circumstances, the choice of 'which afternoon to use for PPA time' has been an easy decision – replace the stressful hour that includes getting children changed for PE and managing the entire class in the hall with office time for marking and literacy planning. If teachers aren't confident enough to teach PE, who can criticise such a choice?

The use of adults other than teachers (AOTTs) to support learning in physical education has now become very commonplace in both primary and secondary schools. A range of individual volunteer and professional coaches has always been active in supporting the subject area and this has escalated since the introduction of PPA time. A plethora of commercial sports coaching organisations now also exist to service this demand, capitalising on headteachers' PPA budget allocation and usually costing less than an equivalent supply teacher. The range of suppliers will also include local authority sports development coaches, community football schemes, professional sportsmen and women and volunteer parents. For some schools, this has been a neat solution for staffing issues in the subject. For others, alarm has been raised, most commonly centred on claims that the educational value of the subject is being undermined by the use of non-qualified teachers. This relates back to earlier discussions regarding physical education and sport and whether or not the wider educational benefits of physical activity are the sole preserve of qualified teachers. Common sense and good practice guidance would suggest, however, that the quality of the learning process (regardless of professional status) is the most critical issue at stake. To this end, it is recommended that such staff are deployed in line with nationally and locally published good practice guidelines (see, for example, SCUK/AfPE, 2006).

PRACTICAL TASK PRACTICAL TASK **PRACTICAL TASK** PRACTICAL TASK **PRACTICAL TASK**

Consider the following scenario.

During your final school-based Initial Teacher Training experience, you are determined to apply your new PE knowledge to a real life teaching situation. You discover, however, that one PE lesson for your class per week is taught by an external coach, and that this tends to be a football session. In the term that you are placed in this school, the second lesson of the week is swimming and this takes place off-site and is taught by a Local Authority instructor.

How would you go about negotiating an opportunity to teach physical education in this setting? Do you feel confident enough to make sure that you have this opportunity?

Extended schools are a further example of the fast changing role of schools in modern England. In this model, schools are charged with providing a range of services outside the teaching curriculum, to improve access to learning opportunities and raise achievement. By 2010, all primary schools should provide access to high-quality childcare, 8am to 6pm, five days a week, 48 weeks a year, based on community need. In addition to this wrap-around care, primary schools should offer access to a range of study support activities, including the following.

- Activities that enable children at the extremes of the learning spectrum to fulfil their potential (colloquially known as 'catch-up' and 'stretch' activities).
- Arts activities such as dance, drama, art and crafts.
- Sports activities, which will contribute to the target of four hours of high-quality PE and school sport per week.

REFLECTIVE TASK

Consider the range of people that work with you in school. Make a list of all your colleagues who are *not* qualified teachers. In PE and school sport, identify any implications for your own practice and discuss these with a colleague.

- Any skills that you need to develop to manage the work of colleagues.
- Any internal systems and policies that should be developed to reflect approaches to staffing.
- Your knowledge of where to seek best practice guidance relating to PE and school sport.
- How the work of colleagues outside the curriculum plays a role in the objectives of your school.
- The practical steps you can put in place to ensure that you are aware of the learning that takes place beyond those lessons for which you are responsible.

Am I really prepared to teach high-quality physical education?

To be an effective primary school physical educator, it is obvious that a teacher must develop knowledge of the moving child, the context within which the child is moving (the specific activity, space or skills required) and the learning that is the focus of such movement experiences. This knowledge is therefore both subject content knowledge and subject specific pedagogical knowledge – both equally important influences on the quality of learning taking place. The subject content of primary physical education is shaped by the curriculum of the day. At the time of writing this chapter (in 2007), the Key Stage 1 and Key Stage 2 Physical Education curriculum has remained unchanged since 1999, despite amendments to the content of the Early Years Foundation Stage for 0–5 year old children and a review of learning at Key Stage 3 (QCA, 2007). At the same time, significant changes to the education system have been seen, brought about through central policy implementation and strategy.

You must take stock of the nature and content of primary physical education. If you have a clear and agreed notion of *what* teaching and learning experiences children should accrue in progressing from early to later childhood, then you have a realistic chance of deciding *how* and by *whom* this learning should be facilitated. It is possible, for example, that a move away from an activity-based curriculum (traditionally based around games, gymnastics and dance activities) towards a framework that includes developmentally-appropriate movement competences may clarify and simplify what many primary practitioners appear most concerned about. Such an approach may also sit better within the prevailing *Every Child Matters* agenda (DfES, 2003a) within which some feel that:

> *beginning teachers need to undergo sustained study of the theoretical perspectives on child development, on human learning, on the environmental and other obstacles to human flourishing, on the conditions which maximise learning, and on the manifold ways in which learning is facilitated and managed.*
>
> (Kirk and Broadhead, 2007: 12)

The preparation of primary class teachers to teach physical education has been the focus of concern among professional bodies and the research community for some time. Most recently, there have been claims that the quantity and quality of some UK-based primary Initial Teacher Training (ITT) are a 'national disgrace' (Talbot, 2007). Research has suggested that primary physical education ITT in the UK can amount to just nine hours (within a one-year Post Graduate Certificate of Education (PGCE) course) and five hours for those involved with School-Centred Initial Teacher Training (Caldecott et al., 2006a; 2006b).

A succession of studies relating to subject-specific training for primary teachers have repeatedly confirmed that many teachers enter the profession lacking the subject knowledge and confidence to effectively deliver the physical education Curriculum (see, for example, Physical Education Association, 1984; Williams, 1985; Carney and Armstrong, 1996; Morgan, 1997; Clay, 1999; Warburton, 2001). While it is fair to say that personal competence and subject knowledge across six activity areas provide a particular challenge to teachers who may be more comfortable working in a classroom context, it would be wrong to assume that such issues have only arisen since the introduction of an activity-based National Curriculum via the Educational Reform Act of 1988. As long ago as 1969, Rains suggested that there was a lack of a common policy for the preparation of primary teachers in physical education, while over thirty years ago Saunders (1975) suggested that some primary teachers were personally disinterested in physical activity, holding a negative attitude towards the subject – a view that has since been supported by a series of studies in the UK and in other contexts (see, for example, Portman, 1996; Xiang et al., 2002).

Deeper investigations relating to perceptions of personal competence and links to personal biographies have revealed a wide range of training needs for those embarking on careers as primary class teachers (see, for example, Morgan and Bourke, 2005). While some trainees enter the profession as enthusiasts for physical education, others appear to seek opportunities to avoid teaching the subject. In whatever way the allotted time for preparation in PE is used during ITT, it is perhaps impossible to cater for such a diverse range of training needs within a 'one-size-fits-all' model, particularly as session time appears to be so limited. It would appear also that college-based content struggles to provide opportunities for trainees to investigate and analyse personal biographies, values, beliefs or embodied practices, thought to be a particularly important exercise where prior experiences provide primary trainees with negative perceptions of the subject (highlighted by Howarth, 1987; Allison et al., 1990; Garrett and Wrench, 2007).

In light of all this, the primary physical educator surely needs to have a knowledge and understanding that relate specifically to children's motor development and how learning in the physical context is best framed to promote learning in all developmental domains. The development of subject knowledge and pedagogy for all primary practitioners can surely start from such a premise that is regardless of one's status as class teacher or PE specialist – or as a teaching assistant or peripatetic coach, for that matter.

So, in the face of a long history of concern around the preparation of primary teachers to deliver PE, it would appear that something must be done to improve their lot and consequently the experiences of children in today's schools. What exactly this 'something' should be is where debate must centre. Alexander (1992) previously considered broad possibilities for the primary profession and suggested that practitioners held a:

> *sense that the generalist model of primary school staffing has reached its limits: the alternatives are neither clear nor proven. Certainly it would be a grave mistake to replace one monolithic model by another.*
>
> (p 205)

If this is the case, then surely the remodeled workforce should provide a golden opportunity for flexible staffing that will help to ensure a high quality of experience for all children.

Can physical education cure the world's ills?

Bold claims have frequently been made on behalf of the subject. For example, the International Year for Education through Sport claimed that the subject could be seen as 'a means to promote education, health, development and peace' (United Nations, 2003, 58/19). A recent academic review conducted by the British Education Research Association (Bailey et al., 2007) has however confirmed the need to be cautious. It would appear that the scientific evidence base for claims regarding the educational benefits of physical education and sport is pretty thin. This is not to say that positive relationships between physical education and sport and developmental domains (i.e. physical, social, cognitive, and social) do not exist . . . it is more that causal links are yet to be established. It is fair to say however, that physical education in schools and sport in the community, for *some* children and young people, in *some* circumstances, at *some* times, can have a positive impact – in *some* cases leading to very significant social empowerment and change.

A focus on developing a more coherent evidence base also has an element of self-preservation attached. Where national policies are increasingly target based, a new and challenging level of accountability is being felt by teachers and educational managers in this context. For example, in England, where policy has recently been geared to deliver against specific objectives (known as Public Sector Agreements), failure to meet centrally imposed targets could lead to withdrawal of funding and a reduction in subject status. The rising body weight of children continues to grab headlines, so much so that the government has set a specific target to 'halt the year on year rise in obesity amongst children under 11 by 2010 in the context of a broader strategy to tackle obesity in the population as a whole' (HM Treasury, 2004).

This example has raised significant debate in the UK, particularly in relation to the perceived relationship between primary school physical education and childhood obesity. The setting of numeric targets is problematic in education and community sport, where the outcomes of schooling are as much to do with individual feelings, moods and behaviours as they are to do with statistics. If the health agenda becomes the main driving force behind PE and the central tenet of individual teacher's rationales for the subject, then a curriculum model based around physical activity and exercise will be the likely future structure. The recently appointed Prime Minister, Gordon Brown, has been quick to reaffirm his government's commitment to school sport by announcing extended investment to ensure all children and young people are able to access five hours of sport each week. Is this commitment driven by a wish to create more elite sports performers, or a healthier nation, or for the value of movement as an educative vehicle to be promoted?

So at a time when the research community has acknowledged the need for greater evidence regarding the efficacy of physical education and sport, politicians continue to promote, advocate and set targets. The PE community must come together to ensure that the significant status attached to PE and sport across the world is not undermined or hijacked by those who make unsubstantiated claims. Failure to meet local targets or perhaps to promote 'world peace' may eventually result in the erosion of the headline grabbing status that is currently enjoyed.

PRACTICAL TASK PRACTICAL TASK **PRACTICAL TASK** PRACTICAL TASK **PRACTICAL TASK**

1. Consider the class of children who you are currently teaching. Do they fit with the populist view that children are getting fatter? Do you think that any of the children are overweight/obese? If you can answer 'yes' to this question, how would you plan to work with these children and their families, and colleagues in and outside school, to tackle this issue? Do you consider this part of your role as a physical educator?

2. Consider how you could measure the impact of your own physical education teaching in a specific developmental domain. If you think that PE can foster self-esteem, promote social cohesion, or develop thinking skills, how do you *know*? Work with a colleague to develop this into an action research project and share your findings with other colleagues.

How can I deliver high quality and inclusive PE?

Whatever level of funding is made available for PE and school sport, and whatever perceived status exists, the quality of this experience is only as strong as the people charged with delivering it. For every child and young person to experience truly high-quality physical education and sport, a workforce must be developed who knows what this looks like, knows how to deliver it and is supported in doing so with the relevant resources and facilities. This is an area where the profession has much work to do and despite the best efforts of the PESSCL strategy there are significant weaknesses in this regard. For example, Initial Teacher Training of primary teachers has been described recently by Margaret Talbot, Chief Executive of the association for PE, as a 'national disgrace' – no wonder then that many primary headteachers are happy to allow non-qualified teachers to deliver curriculum PE. A new workforce has thus emerged, allowed into schools as part of the 'remodelled agenda', and who may or may not be equipped with the skills to deliver a high-quality PE curriculum. This is an area of significant concern and will only be solved by a coming together of educational and sports professionals to develop a system through which any practitioner working with children meets specific qualification and experience criteria. The time has passed for these requirements to meet 'minimum operating standards' and the benchmark needs to be significantly raised for the benefit of *all* children and young people. The focus of efforts in physical education must clearly be on assurance of quality and inclusion.

So, what exactly do we mean by *high quality physical education?* Definitions of high-quality have been developed by the DfES and QCA as part of the PESSCL strategy and these very helpfully focus on outcomes demonstrated by those learners who have experienced this quality. However, the PESSCL target of raising amount and quality of PE teaching has proved difficult to measure: self-administered questionnaires to show designated curriculum time are very straightforward compared to making judgments about quality.

This by definition is rather subjective and relative to the existing practice apparent in a school. For example, does high-quality mean that PE lessons are never cancelled for other activities in the hall, or that assessment for learning, informed by detailed movement observation, is embedded in delivery to ensure every learner is working at an appropriate level? For high-quality physical education to exist, do teachers need to have good or excellent subject knowledge and do teachers need to know how to use two (or ten) different teaching strategies? The answers to these questions should bring the focus back to the specific and individual context within which you work. Whether you utilise QCA definitions or Ofsted inspection criteria to benchmark your own practice and that of colleagues, the key factor to base judgments on must be the amount and rate of pupil learning demonstrated by all children.

PRACTICAL TASK PRACTICAL TASK PRACTICAL TASK PRACTICAL TASK PRACTICAL TASK

Work with a group of colleagues to create a list of up to ten factors that you would like to use as indicators of quality in your own physical education teaching. Compare your list with that of others – what are the differences? Rationalise your lists to agree on one and negotiate the opportunity to team-teach with a colleague. During part of this lesson, spend time observing your colleague and consider the extent to which the lesson is high-quality. Make sure that you spend time following the lesson to discuss this further with each other and to consider how you might make changes to your practice.

And what about *inclusive physical education*? Fully inclusive PE will cater for the learning needs of all children, regardless of age, stage of development, skill level, height, weight, ethnicity, gender, disability, social class, and so on. Beginning the planning process for physical education from the starting point of 'every child is different' will stand you in good stead; many of the perceived barriers to physical activity and sport in society are socially created and the final barrier to all pupils engaging fully with the physical education learning process is often created by teachers themselves. Providing appropriate equipment (size, weight, colour, etc.) and designing appropriate tasks are part and parcel of teaching high quality PE and the approach is the same whether catering for diverse physical needs or a range of cognitive abilities. In some parts of the world, *adapted physical education* is used to describe physical education that caters for the needs of specific learners (such as those in wheelchairs or with specific disabilities). A more inclusive approach would be to say that *all* physical education is adapted in that the differentiation of tasks meets the precise learning needs of every learner. The barriers to learning are all too often created by teachers who expect all learners to progress at the same rate and to take part in exactly the same activities. It would appear, however, that we are currently a long way from creating a fully inclusive approach to physical education and sport. It is scandalous, for example, to note that current levels of physical activity and sport among young disabled people in London are significantly lower than amongst non-disabled peers (LSF, 2007).

REFLECTIVE TASK
REFLECTIVE TASK

1. With a colleague, consider the range of learning needs that your current class demonstrates in PE. Write a list of all the different labels that could be attached to children in your class to show that they have a specific need. This could range from a specific disability to a more subjective label.
2. Can you say whether or not your current teaching and learning are fully inclusive?
3. Use the list to consider what actions you have to take to make your own teaching inclusive – i.e. ensuring that all learners can fully engage with the tasks and make progress.

What will primary physical education look like in the future?

According to Pickup and colleagues (2007) physical education in the primary years is now more important than ever before. There is a strong sense that the prevailing policy land-scape is providing a context within which the importance of the health and well-being of children cannot be ignored. Although the research base in primary PE remains relatively thin, practitioners should feel empowered by current agendas to promote, utilise and celebrate the PE curriculum and extra curricular sport activities. The recent investment through the PESSCL strategy has provided a once in a lifetime opportunity for those involved with the subject to seize, and every primary school teacher should now be a part of this.

Including all children and young people in a *lifelong* framework of physical education, sport, physical activity and healthy lifestyles is not only desirable, it is the *only* possible course of action. It has been suggested that for some children the school context provides their only opportunity for physical learning and as such is vital if children are to develop physical skills that will enable them to access physical activity, recreation and sporting opportunities throughout life. Experiences in the primary years can help to provide this foundation and can foster an intrinsic motivation to be active. Being physically active should be a pleasur-able experience and one that we would like young people to seek out – primary physical education should therefore aim to engage all children in fun and relevant activities with a view to these being connected to experiences across the lifespan.

The development of curricula that simultaneously advocate a *lifewide* approach should also be a priority where experiences in school, home, community and other settings are of equal worth. This quality of experience should not be governed by notions of talent or geogra-phical factors. In other words, we must be able to guarantee that all children, regardless of social class, race, gender or physical ability gain the highest possible calibre of experience in settings where physical activity and sport are the focus. This requires all primary school teachers to become advocates of PE and physical activity and to guarantee that opportu-nities for teaching and learning in the subject area are fully utilised. It then follows that (if primary physical education is to become part of a planned-for lifelong process and is to be relevant across the breadth of lived experiences for all children) a strong emphasis must be placed on planning in detail and in the long term. Planning individual lesson plans in isolated units does not necessarily provide the required levels of 'joined-upness'; progression and continuity of learning within year groups, across key stages, between schools and into community sports clubs can and should be planned for. This can only be provided by teachers who recognise the need to connect lessons in this way and who are willing to lead change in physical education in their own contexts. While the need for each teacher or coach to plan individual lessons from week to week remains, it is vital that this does not take place in a vacuum. A subject leader in PE must therefore develop a keen understanding of the broad physical learning landscape that is in play in their community and must work with colleagues to maximise opportunities for all children.

Records of pupils' learning need not be confined to tick lists and written reports – the colourful and dynamic world of physical education is well suited to the use of ICT (particularly video and digital imagery) as a means of recording and demonstrating learning and it is now possible for parents, community sports coaches and leisure centre staff to be aware of the abilities (and learning needs) of children. Similarly, teachers must also value the significant learning that takes place in such non-school settings and should communicate effectively with other professionals to ensure that their own lessons are planned to meet children's specific needs.

It is likely that the focus and content of future statutory curricula will be different to existing frameworks. In the UK today there is significant interest in developing new approaches to physical education (particularly in the primary years), largely centred on broadening the content away from prescribed 'activity areas' towards a focus on fundamental movement skill development and what some call 'physical literacy' (see Whitehead, 2006). There is also much scope for making learning opportunities more individually relevant and for engaging children more fully in decision-making processes. Whatever the content of primary PE in years to come, it is essential that it is delivered and facilitated by committed and knowledgeable professionals, fully prepared to work with children aged from 3 to 11 years old, and who are able to make the connections to wider learning opportunities for all children.

REFLECTIVE TASK

This section has suggested that primary PE should be:

- part of a lifelong process;
- part of a lifewide process;
- inclusive of all children.

Consider your most recent school-based experience and the extent to which the PE taught reflects these aims. How would you change the focus of your own teaching or even the curriculum frameworks in the future to ensure that these aims are met?

A SUMMARY OF **KEY POINTS**

While the status of physical education and sport appears to be high, in part fuelled by the media attention directed at professional sport and in part by mass hysteria regarding the health of our populations, this status should not be confused with a more important concern for quality and inclusion. Prevailing educational policy is leading the profession towards joined-up thinking and increasingly interdisciplinary working habits, which include opportunities for increased investment and professional development. If we are really serious about improving the health and well-being of children, primary PE must be seen to be more important than ever before.

Every effort must be made for the physical education and sports communities to come together within coherent, joined-up approaches that value participation, performance, physical activity, physical education and sport in equal measure. Policy must be based upon on an evidence base garnered through rigorous scientific enquiry. Practitioners should be supported to deliver high quality experiences both through initial training and on-going professional development. Crucially, all sections of the professional community should work together to decide what 'quality' looks and feels like for those young people who are experiencing it. Without this, any status derived from politicians and funding bodies will be for nothing.

The context within which teaching takes place is constantly shifting as society and its norms develop. High-quality teaching and learning in primary PE will therefore also change and curriculums will continually be in a state of flux. The key is for individual teachers to remain committed to facilitating learning in and through the physical and to embrace the possibilities that present themselves for PE to play a major role in child development in the twenty-first century. Committed individual teachers must also be supported by dynamic and passionate leadership in each school and it is this workforce that must itself be empowered by headteachers, government and funding bodies. Ensuring that every child has access to physical education is now merely a minimum standard – we must surely strive for the highest quality of experience for all children and in some cases this may require a radical rethink of the way the subject is taught.

REFERENCES REFERENCES **REFERENCES** REFERENCES **REFERENCES** REFERENCES

Alexander, R. (1992) *Policy and Practice in Primary Education*, Abingdon: Routledge.

Allison, P. C., Pissanos, B.W. and Sakola, S. P. (1990) Physical education revisited—the institutional biographies of preservice classroom teachers, *Journal of Physical Education, Recreation and Dance*, 61(5): 76–79.

Bailey, R., Armour, K., Kirk, D., Jess, M., Pickup, I., Sandford, R. and the BERA Physical Education and Sport Pedagogy Special Interest Group (in press) The Educational benefits Claimed for Physical Education and School Sport: An Academic review, *Research Papers in Education*.

Bailey, R., Doherty, J. and Pickup, I. (2007) *Physical Development and Physical Education, in J. Riley (ed.) Learning in the early years* (2nd ed), p.167–199, London: Sage.

Caldecott, S., Warburton, P. and Waring, M. (2006a) 'A survey of the time devoted to the preparation of primary and junior school trainee teachers to teach Physical Education in England', *The British Journal of Teaching Physical Education*, 37(1): 45–48.

Caldecott, S., Warburton, P. and Waring, M. (2006b) 'A survey of the time devoted to the preparation of primary and junior school trainee teachers to teach Physical Education in England', *Physical Education Matters,* 1(1): 45–48.

Carney, C. and Armstrong, N. (1996) 'The provision of Physical Education in primary Initial Teacher Training courses in England and Wales', *European Physical Education Review*, 2(1): 64–74.

DfES (2003) *Excellence and Enjoyment: a strategy for primary schools*. London: DfES.

DfES (2004) *Children Act*. London: HMSO.

Educational Reform Act (1988) *Education Reform Act*. London: HMSO.

Garbarino, J. (1998) 'Raising children in a socially toxic environment', *Australian Institute of Family Studies, Family Matters* 50: 53–55.

Garrett, R. and Wrench, A. (2007) 'Physical experiences: primary student teachers' conceptions of sport and physical education', *Physical Education and Sport Pedagogy*, 12 (1): 23–42.

HM Treasury (2004) *2004 Spending Review PSA*. London: HM Treasury.

Howarth, K. (1987) 'Initial training in primary physical education – no substitute for teamwork', *British Journal of Physical Education*, 18(4): 152–153.

Kay, W. (2003) 'Physical Education, R.I.P?', *British Journal of Teaching Physical Education*, 34 (4): 6-10.

Kirk, G. and Broadhead, P. (2007) *Every Child Matters and Teacher Education: a UCET position paper*. London: UCET.

London Sports Forum (2007) *Inclusive and Active, A Sport and Physical Activity Action Plan for Disabled People in London*. London: Greater London Authority.

Morgan, I. (1997) 'The preparation of Physical Education teachers during Initial Teacher Training', *The British Journal of Teaching Physical Education*, 28(3): 18–20.

Morgan, P. J. and Bourke, S. F. (2005) 'An investigation of preservice and primary school teachers' perspectives of PE teaching confidence and PE teacher education', *ACHPER Healthy Lifestyles Journal*, 52 (1): 7–13.

Physical Education Association (PEA) (1987) *Report of a Commission of Enquiry, Physical Education in Schools*. London: PEA.

Pickup, I., Haydn-Davies, D. and Jess, M. (2007) 'The importance of primary physical education', *Physical Education Matters*, 2 (1): 8–11.

Portman, P.A. (1996) 'Preservice elementary education majors beliefs about their elementary physical education classes (Pt. 1)', *Indiana Association for Health, PE, Recreation and Dance Journal,* 25 (2): 25–28.

QCA (2007) *Programme of Study for Key Stage 3 and attainment target*. London: QCA.

Rains, M. (1969) 'Professional training for primary teachers in Physical Education'. Unpublished MEd thesis, University of Leicester.

Speednet (2000) 'Primary school Physical Education – Speednet survey makes depressing reading', *British Journal of Physical Education*, 30 (30): 19–20.

Sports Coach UK (2007) *The UK Coaching Framework: A 3-7-11 Year Action Plan*. Leeds: Sports Coach UK.

Sports Coach UK/Association for Physical Education (2006) *School Induction Pack for Adults Supporting Learning (Including Coaches and Volunteers): A Framework for Development*, Leeds: Coachwise.

Talbot, M. (2007) 'Quality', *Physical Education Matters*, 2 (2): 12.

United Nations (2003) Resolution adopted by the General Assembly: 58/5: *Sport as a means to promote education, health, development and peace*.

Whitehead, M. (2006) Physical Literacy and Physical Education: Conceptual Mapping, *Physical Education Matters* 1, (1), 6–9.

Williams, E. (1985) 'Perspectives on Initial Teacher Training in Physical Education for primary school teachers', in: *The 28th ICHPER World Congress proceedings,* West London Institute for Higher Education, 29 July–3 August: 726–734.

Xiang, P., Lowy, S., and McBride, R. (2002) 'The impact of a field-based elementary physical education methods course on preservice classroom teachers' beliefs', *Journal of Teaching in Physical Education,* 21(2): 145–161.

FURTHER READING FURTHER READING **FURTHER READING** FURTHER READING

ATL, DfES, GMB, NAHT, NASUWT, NEOST, PAT, SHA, TGWU, UNISON, WAG (2003) *Raising Standards and Tracking Workload: A National Agreement*. Accessed via www.remodelling.org, June 2006.

Bailey, R., Kirk, D., Jess, M., Sandford, R., Pickup, I. and Armour, K. (in press) *The Educational Value of Physical education and Sport*. Aldershot: BERA.

Clay, G. (1999) 'Movement backwards and forwards: the influence of government on PE – an HMI perspective', *The British Journal of Physical Education*, 30(4): 38–41.

Curtner-Smith, M.D. (1998) 'Influence of biography, teacher education, and entry into the workforce on the perspectives and practises of first-year elementary school physical education teachers',

European Journal of Physical Education, (3): 75–98.

DCSF (2007a) *The Children's Plan: Building Brighter Futures*. London: DCSF.

DCSF (2007) *Extended Schools: Building on experience*. London: DCSF.

DfES/DCMS (2003) *Learning Through PE and Sport – a guide to the Physical Education, School Sport and Club Links Strategy*. Annesley: DfES.

DfES (2003) *Every Child Matters*. London: DfES.

Jess, M., Pickup, I. and Haydn-Davies, D. (2007) 'Physical Education in the primary school: a developmental, inclusive and connected future', *Physical Education Matters*, 2 (1): 16–20.

Lacey, C. (1977) *The Socialization of Teachers*. London: Methuen.

Marsden, E. and Weston, C. (2007) 'Locating quality physical education in early years pedagogy', *Sport, Education and Society*, 12 (4): 383–398.

Palmer, S. (2006) *Toxic Childhood: How The Modern World Is Damaging Our Children And What We Can Do About It*. London: Orion.

Poulson, L. (2001) 'Paradigm lost? Subject knowledge, primary teachers and education policy, *British Journal of Educational Studies*, 49 (1): 40–55.

Price, A. and Willett, J. (2006) 'Primary teachers' perceptions of the impact of Initial Teacher Training upon primary schools', *Journal of In-service Education,* 32 (1): 33–45.

Saunders, R. (1975) 'A case for the physical education specialist in the primary school'. Paper presented at the *Madeley College of Education Physical Education Conference – Teaching Physical Education Today and Tomorrow.*

Wainwright, N. (2006) 'Accessing learning through effective Physical Education', *Physical Education Matters*, 1 (3).

Warburton, P. (2001) 'A sporting future for all: fact or fiction?', *The British Journal of Teaching Physical Education*, 32(2): 18–21.

Williams, E. (1985) 'Perspectives on Initial Teacher Training in Physical Education for primary school teachers', in: *The 28th ICHPER World Congress proceedings,* West London Institute for Higher Education, 29 July–3 August: 726–734.

Xiang, P., Lowy, S., and McBride, R. (2002) 'The impact of a field-based elementary physical education methods course on preservice classroom teachers' beliefs', *Journal of Teaching in Physical Education,* 21(2): 145–161.

5

Health and Safety: guidelines for good practice, resources to support teaching and learning in PE
Julie Shaughnessy

By the end of this chapter you will have an understanding of:

- **what is meant by safe practice;**
- **the importance of developing a framework for safe practice within teaching and learning in PE;**
- **safety principles within lesson preparation, including resources and equipment;**
- **how to develop safe management within lessons.**

This chapter addresses, and makes a contribution to, the following Professional Standards for QTS:

- **Professional attributes – Q3(a) Q3(b)**
- **Health and well-being – Q21 (a)**
- **Teaching – Q25 (d)**
- **Assessment, monitoring and giving feedback – Q26 (b)**

Introduction

The concept of safety should be a priority throughout the planning and delivery of physical education lessons. This is because, of all the curricula subjects, physical education probably has the greatest potential for creating situations where accidents resulting in bodily injury can occur.

(Bailey and Macfayden, 2000: 100)

Teachers need to plan not just for the content of lessons but also for the learning context. As highlighted in Chapter 1 the emphasis within high-quality PE is for learners to share in the learning process, which focuses on learning from meaningful participation and developing understanding of movement. In the primary years, children should engage within PE activities with increasing independence and become more knowledgeable about movement concepts (Pickup and Price, 2007). Embedded within developing understanding of the curriculum and pedagogy are concepts about moving safely and procedures for safe practice. These ensure that children understand about safety and that the teacher prepares effectively to encompass a framework for safe practice within lessons. Moving does, however, contain risk and we need to be mindful of the potential risks that physical activity can pose and embed procedures to manage risk to support the development of safe environments for learning. Raymond (1998: 21) reminds us that 'there is risk in almost everything we do and that safety cannot be guaranteed or ensured because of unforeseen conditions, improper decisions and poor judgment, can all generate risk or hazard'. A school, therefore, requires a policy to manage the environment and importantly they must operate within a legal frame-work.

What do we mean by safe practice?

Within PE the importance of children moving safely with control and confidence, and building resilience and understanding of the principles and concepts which keep children safe in their work, is an integral part of learning to move. Alongside this are the important professional responsibilities a teacher has in operating a *duty of care* for children within PE lessons. There is also the recognition that the PE curriculum presents the teacher with a range of activity areas, (games, dance, gymnastics, swimming, athletics and outdoor and adventurous activities), each in a range of different localities with specific safety considerations. Awareness of safety and developing frameworks for safe practice therefore are integral to teaching and learning within physical education. The British Association for Advisers and Lecturers in Physical Education (BAALPE) (2004) has developed safe practice guidelines that highlight the importance of teachers being prepared and aware of the risks involved within activities. Integral to this is preparation in ensuring that children are also prepared through the process of their learning within PE to manage their bodies with care and control and to understand their own safety when working alone and with others.

Safety, therefore, involves children developing, knowledge of themselves as movers and understanding how to move with control and resilience. It also involves important health concepts including how to warm up and cool down; developing body awareness; using the space; the planning and appraisal of surfaces and working with others.

Staying safe and the importance of the school providing a safe environment for learning are key outcomes of the Children Act (1989) as expressed through *Every Child Matters* (DfES, 2003). Local authorities as well as school governing bodies alongside subject co-ordinators and individual teachers have collective responsibility in establishing safe practice across schools. Developing a policy for safe practice is therefore a whole-school issue. This involves understanding both the legal and professional responsibilities.

Legal responsibilities

As the BAALPE (2004) Safe Practice Guidelines make clear all schools are required to have a formal Health and Safety Policy which should be regularly reviewed. A safe practice policy for PE would normally be developed alongside this, based on the specific requirements of the subject. The National Curriculum for Physical Education (1999), also requires that the risk assessment process is taught to children and that they should receive clear guidance and experience to enable them to develop their own knowledge and understanding of safe practice.

The law expects that all teachers working in PE will do so within a *duty of care* (BAALPE, 2004) which requires teachers to:

- identify foreseeable risks that may result in injury;
- take reasonably practicable steps to reduce the risk to an acceptable level.

These responsibilities are outlined in a range of documents cited by BAALPE (2004), including the following.

Acts of Parliament
- The Health and Safety at Work Act 1974 (HSWA).
- The Occupiers' Liability Acts 1957 and 1984.
- The Children Act 1989.
- The Protection of Children Act 1999 (POCA).
- The Activity Centres (Young Persons' Safety) Act 1995.
- The Special Educational Needs and Disability and Discrimination Act 2001.

Regulations
- The Adventure Activities Licensing Regulations 2004.
- The Management of Health and Safety at Work Regulations 1999.
- The Reporting of Injuries, Diseases and Dangerous Occurrences Regulations 1995 (RIDDOR).
- The Provision and Use of Work Equipment Regulations 1998.
- The Education (Specified Work Registration) (England) Regulations 2003.

The legal responsibilities stipulated within the Health and Safety at Work Act (1974), require employers, local authorities, governing bodies and managers to ensure that everything is reasonably practicable to ensure the health and safety of employees (teachers and other support staff) and non-employees (children, parents and other visitors to the school premises). Part of the duty of care under the terms of Section 2(3) of the Health and Safety at Work Act (1974) is that employers are required to prepare (and revise):

- a written statement containing a general policy to the health and safety of employees;
- guidelines on its implementation;
- and must inform their employees about the statement and any revision of it.

As Pickup and Price (2007: 203) highlight a school PE Health and Safety Policy contained within the overarching health and safety policy should include:

- a statement stressing the importance of health and safety and stressing the legal duty of care;
- an informed statement that explains the educational value of the challenge and the need to 'manage' risk;
- specific activity guidelines which include procedures and routines for specific pieces of equipment or certain environments;
- guidelines that outline procedures for the care and maintenance of facilities and equipment, to include spaces used for PE. It is advisable to remind all colleagues of their own duty to report damaged or faulty equipment as part of normal operating procedures;
- an explanation of the school policy regarding the use of voluntary or employed helpers who are not qualified teachers;
- guidance regarding planning formats and the use of assessment to determine pupils' learning needs in particular activities;
- the school's commitment to on-going staff development;
- details of the school's insurance policy.

Risk assessment

The management and identification of risk are essential parts of a teacher's duty. Effective risk assessment procedures set out a series of strategies and procedures for teachers to follow through which identify the potential hazards and consider measures that can be put into place to prevent the possibility of accidents occurring. The Management of Health and

Safety at Work (1999) regulations set down guidelines for planning, organising, controlling, monitoring and reviewing the arrangements that they make for health and safety. Part of these involves headteachers and governing bodies undertaking risk assessments to identify the levels of risk and ensure that risks are appropriately managed. Risk assessments are therefore central to any health and safety system. All risk assessments should, according to BAALPE (2004), cover the following.

People
- Any staff, volunteers and paid coaches involved (i.e competence, experience and training).
- Any children involved (abilities, previous experience, behaviour and individual needs).

Context
- The nature of the activity.
- The premises.
- The equipment.
- The procedures for a safe working environment.

Organisation
- Preparation – through planning and assessment of hazards.
- Teaching style and class organisation.

In addition, consideration should be given to minimising or removing hazards and ensuring that the process in place for managing risk and conducting risk assessment is documented over time. This ensures that the review of the health and safety process is clearly documented and can be reflected upon.

The Health and Safety Executive, in their document 'Managing Health and Safety' (1995) and cited in Severs et al. (2003), considers the function of teachers and managers. In summary, there are four important areas for the class teacher.

- Follow the policy and set guidelines.
- Check the work areas and equipment are safe.
- Participate in inspections and risk assessments.
- Report any problems to the subject leader/PE co-ordinator.

REFLECTIVE TASK

Using the summary of the BAALPE (2004: 100) guidance, reflect on the following areas that are important for effective risk management.

People
- Children are involved in the assessment and management of the risks involved.
- Children should show care and respect for physical education facilities.
- Children should be able to handle physical education equipment safely and recognise the importance in doing so.
- School staff should be familiar with school policies on the safe use and maintenance of the physical education environment.

Context

- All facilities should be subject to a regular maintenance programme (e.g. cleaning and ensuring that they are safe for purpose).
- Equipment should generally only be used for the purpose for which it was designed.
- Arrangements should be made for all physical education equipment to be inspected, maintained and repaired on an annual basis.

Organisation

- All school staff, volunteers and coaches (and pupils where appropriate) should be aware of the action to take if physical education equipment or facilities become unsafe.

Duty of care

In operating duty of care it is expected that 'a teacher must take such care as would a reasonably prudent parent in the same situation as the teacher' (Lyes *v.* Middlesex County Council, 1962, cited in BAALPE (2004)). Reminding us of the professional issues, Raymond (1998) notes that parents and the general public often set professional responsibility for children's well-being and safety above that of the parents. As professionals, we must also reflect on our moral responsibilities in ensuring the safety of children within our care and that children participate within purposeful PE. As Severs et al. (2003) highlight these aspects are part of teachers understanding that lessons need to be pitched to suit the children's range of ability and experience and should reflect the requirements laid down in the PE curriculum. Overall, teachers must retain the responsibility for the class and groups of children irrespective of who might be engaged in teaching them (as a sports coach, swimming instructor, etc.) or where the teaching takes place (on-site or off-site). Increasingly, schools are involved with a range of agencies since the introduction of the National Physical Education, School Sport and Clubs Links (PESSCL) strategy in 2003. To support schools the Association for Physical Education AfPE have produced *Best Practice Guidance* (2007) for the effective use of individual agency coaches in PE and school sport. This includes links to the Department for Children, Schools and Families (DCSF) and Sport England's Child Protection in Sport Unit (CPSU).

RESEARCH SUMMARY RESEARCH SUMMARY **RESEARCH SUMMARY** RESEARCH SUMMARY

BEST PRACTICE GUIDANCE ON THE EFFECTIVE USE OF INDIVIDUAL AND AGENCY COACHES IN PHYSICAL EDUCATION AND SCHOOL SPORT (PESS) AfPE (2007)

Headteachers and other managers of coaching support staff are strongly advised to ensure:

1. Safe Recruitment:

a. Arrange a face to face interview with each coach to confirm identity using original documents (passport, driving licence, recent service provider bill confirming current home address);

b. Check CRB enhanced disclosure – see original; decide if portability applies and is acceptable; check with original responsible authority and establish whether additional information is on the CRB form – if so, require a new certificate from the coach to access the additional information. If no response is received to enquiry or information is held a new disclosure certificate is essential;

c. Check qualifications – see originals; accept Level 2 award as normal baseline qualification for each activity the coach is expected to teach, diverting from this standard only if the coach is observed prior to acceptance and demonstrates exceptional coaching qualities and is working towards a Level 2 qualification; refer to the HLTA standards for your baseline (www.hlta.gov.uk) – alternatively check the criteria given in 'The Effective Use of Coaches', AfPE, 2006 (www.afpe.org/healthandsafety);

d. Check training undertaken and experience of working with children and young people – e.g. child protection workshops;

e. Explore motivations to work with children and attitudes towards children and young people;

f. Check reference/s – investigate any gaps in coaching employment, any conditional comments in the reference;

g. Check with relevant National Governing Body that coach is currently licensed to coach (qualification cannot be rescinded but NGB license to coach can be if any poor practice or abuse issues have arisen);

h. Ensure correct employment status and employment rights are known to the coach – provide written summary/include in contract as appropriate;

i. Ensure coach is fully aware of insurance provision and what aspects s/he needs to provide for self (according to employment status) re:

    i. Employers' liability (Compulsory) – legal liability for injuries to employees (permanent/temporary/contracted for services) arising in course of employment;

    ii. Public liability (Essential) – legal responsibility for 'third party' claims against the activities of the individual/group and legal occupation of premises;

    iii. Professional liability (Desirable) – legal cover against claims for breaches of professional duty by employees acting in the scope of their employment, e.g. giving poor professional advice;

    iv. Hirers' liability (Desirable) – covers individuals or agencies that hire premises against any liability for injury to others or damage to the property whilst using it;

    v. Libel and slander insurance (Optional) – cover against claims for defamation, e.g. libellous material in publications, Personal injury – accidental bodily injury – or deliberate assault (Desirable) – arranged by the individual or the employer;

    vii. Miscellaneous – a variety of types of insurance such as travel (Compulsory or Required) or motor insurance (Compulsory) (minimum of 'third party') – check personal exclusions and excesses individual carries;

j. Set out a clearly defined role identifying any limits of responsibility, lines of supervision, management and communication, specialist expertise needed (e.g. children with individual special needs) and ensure they are appropriately qualified/experienced to undertake the role;

k. Determine an agreed period of probation and monitor coach's performance and attitude closely during this period;

l. If an agency coach check that all of above have been addressed by the agency or by the school before the coach begins work;

m. Agree appropriate induction package that must be fulfilled.

2. Induction:

a. Headteacher or their representative to present coach with a summary of relevant school policies and procedures, including: risk assessments, emergency evacuation, referral and incentives, behaviour management, first aid, child protection procedures and something about the ethos of the school – how they work with children and young people (such as looking for success in young people, rewarding achievement};

b. Identified member of staff to manage induction into school procedures who will:

    i. arrange meeting with SENCO (and class teacher/s as appropriate) or other nominated personnel e.g. school sport co-ordinator) for specific information about pupils;

ii.   monitor and assess competency of coach through observations and discussions with pupils and other staff;

iii. determine the coach's role in contributing to the overall assessment of pupils.

3. Qualifications, experience and qualities necessary for coach to work alone:

a. Level 2 award is normal baseline qualification for each activity the coach is expected to teach. Divert from this standard only if the coach is observed prior to acceptance, demonstrates exceptional coaching qualities and is working towards a Level 2 qualification;

b. Check previous experience in working with small/large groups;

c. Check behaviour management skills;

d. Check;

i.   quality of relationships – the way the coach cares for and respects pupils, is an appropriate role model and promotes the ethos of school;

ii. developing knowledge of the pupils – their levels of confidence, ability, individual needs, medical needs and behaviour;

iii. pupil management – how they match pupils' confidence, strength and ability in pair and group tasks, maximise participation, have strategies for effective pupil control and motivation, apply the school's standard procedures and routines – e.g. child protection, emergency action, jewellery, handling and carrying of equipment;

iv. knowledge of the activities – appropriate level of expertise to enable learning to take place in the activity/ies being delivered, use of suitable space for the group, differentiated equipment, differentiated practice, evident progression and application of rules;

v.   observation and analytical skills – providing a safe working and learning environment, ability to identify faults and establish strategies for improvement.

4. Day to day management of coach:

a. Check that the coach has received a summary of school and subject procedures and understands what is required (including clear guidelines in relation to handover of responsibility at the start and end of lessons/ sessions);

b. Ensure the coach receives relevant information on pupils/groups – e.g. illness, family bereavement, behaviour issues;

c. Monitor promptness;

d. Establish regular review and evaluation of coach's work;

e. Determine who assesses pupils' work;

f. Ensure coach is supported, valued and accepted as a member of staff;

g. Monitor dialogue and relationship between class teacher and coach.

5. Monitoring Quality and Effectiveness:

a. Ensure direct monitoring of coach for agreed period – use criteria set out in 3 above;

b. Set up continual indirect monitoring to ensure pupils make progress and enjoy lessons/sessions;

c. Ensure that pupils are engaged in consistent high quality, challenging and stimulating activities that support them to achieve their potential, not just activities that keep them 'busy, happy and good' pupils who do not demonstrate high quality (see DfES *High Quality Physical Education*, 2003).

6. Identification and provision of continuing professional development:

a. Evaluate coach's abilities against HLTA standards;

b. Arrange attendance on AfPE/sports coach UK ASL induction course;

c. Agree essential qualifications and desirable qualifications – plan and provide for personal development programme beyond NGB coach qualifications to enable coach to proceed from emerging to established, and advanced rating.

7. Dealing with inadequate performance by the coach:

a. Proactively monitor coach's work as set out in 5 above;

b. Where performance is inadequate and poses a health and safety risk to the pupils or has the potential to impact on their welfare intervene immediately, where performance is technically inadequate then review situation with coach after the lesson;

c. Agree and provide supportive continuing professional development to improve inadequate aspects of performance;

d. Monitor for improvement;

e. Where little or no improvement occurs then terminate short-term contract or initiate competency procedures if longer-term contract;

f. Where necessary terminate longer-term contract where competence does not improve.

Professional responsibilities

The *School Teachers' Pay and Conditions* Document 2007 references the School Teachers' Pay and Conditions Act (1991) setting out professional guidance on the importance of teachers safeguarding health and safety. You must be aware of the requirements under the duty of care as noted above. As a teacher you have the responsibility to make sure you are up to date and informed and that you continue to reference both specific and general advice on the care and safety of children supported by the Department for Children, Schools and Families through TeacherNet.

As emphasised, the importance of a school's Health and Safety Policy and seeking support from the BAALPE safety guidance documents and advice from professional bodies such as the Physical Education Association (AfPE) is crucial. Within this the importance of professional diligence and systematic monitoring is imperative with respect to safe practice. The monitoring of safety also involves raising the awareness of the children through the learning process where they become increasingly aware of their bodies and their environment and are involved in reflecting upon aspects of safety throughout their physical education. The National Curriculum in Physical Education (NCPE) reflects the importance of embedding safety principles as integral to learning. While safety is emphasised, the importance of the teacher's role in understanding the importance of safety principles and integrating safety as a key process within teaching and learning is vital for effective practice. As Severs et al. (2003) highlight every teacher needs to be aware of what might be termed as *standard* or *good* or 'Regular and Approved' practice. They provide an extensive checklist of 16 key considerations.

RESEARCH SUMMARY RESEARCH SUMMARY **RESEARCH SUMMARY** RESEARCH SUMMARY

Checklist for 'Regular and Approved' Practice adapted from Severs et al. (2003)

1. The form and content of the lesson should reflect what is seen to be standard practice for pupils of the same age across the country.

2. The lesson content should be appropriate to the range of ability and levels of experience of the children and reflect the requirements in the PE policy.

3. Record keeping should be kept on the material covered in lessons and the progress of children including levels of ability, medical conditions, disability and the limits of a child's capability.

4. Levels of supervision must be satisfactory.

5. Those responsible for teaching the lesson must be properly qualified.

6. Support staff such as classroom assistants must be fully briefed and have the necessary knowledge of safety, accident procedures and risk. Support staff should on no account be allowed to adopt an active teaching role e.g. task setting or telling children to attempt particular kinds of movements. Properly trained coaches or instructors who have been engaged by the school or LA may be responsible for lesson content but their roles must be fully agreed with the teacher. The teacher *will always* have overall responsibility for the children and the conduct of the lesson.

7. Teachers must not leave areas whilst activities are taking place *under their control* unless another qualified teacher is present. In an emergency, children should always stop work immediately and sit or stand where they can be seen and away from apparatus or equipment. Responsible children or class assistants or volunteers may be sent for assistance.

8. All equipment should be in good condition and where appropriate properly positioned and secured.

9. The context (and operating conditions) must be free from danger (e.g. slippery or uneven surface).

10. Staff and children should be appropriately dressed and prepared for the lesson.

11. In the absence of medical evidence or to the contrary, children suffering from injuries or who show signs of illness should not take part.

12. The school Health and Safety Policy must include PE and show that the risk assessments have been made and regularly updated. The document should also show those who are responsible for undertaking the assessment and when regular checks should be made and by whom.

13. It is vital that the school has, and parents are informed of, a policy on physical contact with pupils (e.g. supporting gymnastics work).

14. All teachers should be aware of the content of the school's PE policy documents and be absolutely clear on their own responsibilities.

15. Lessons should be planned and along with schemes of work, should make clear reference to safety precautions and minimising risks.

16. Any changes in regard to risk management should be communicated to teachers immediately they are made and checks carried out to ensure the message has been received. Staff should have opportunities to undertake in-service training in risk management and discuss practice and procedures through staff meetings.

REFLECTIVE TASK

Thinking about your current school, or most recent placement, reflect on the key features *Checklist for 'Regular and Approved' Practice* above. Make notes on what provision is in place and what areas need to be highlighted.

PRACTICAL TASK PRACTICAL TASK **PRACTICAL TASK** PRACTICAL TASK **PRACTICAL TASK**

To add to the conclusions you have drawn from the above exercise, conduct an audit of the Health and Safety Policy. What can you deduce from these two exercises that identifies the priorities for the school and priorities for your professional practice?

Learning objective: To increase your understanding of the current Health and Safety Policy for PE in your school. Using the checklist below respond to the questions with support from the PE co-ordinator or an experienced colleague.

Auditing the Health and Safety Policy

- What does the Health and Safety Policy say about PE?
- What does the Health and Safety Policy say about legal duty of care?
- What references are made to the management of risk?
- What specific activity guidelines are there in place for PE?
- What procedures and routines are in place for specific pieces of equipment or certain environments?
- What guidelines are in place for the care and maintenance of facilities and equipment?
- What is the school policy regarding the use of voluntary or employed helpers who are not qualified teachers?
- What guidance is in place regarding planning formats and the use of assessment to determine pupils' learning needs in particular activities?

The importance of developing a framework for safe practice within teaching and learning in PE

Many teachers have concerns about safety within PE. The range both of activities and of contexts brings to the fore an array of teaching considerations. Sometimes teachers place very tight, regimented routines in place which ensure the control of movement within the lesson but lead to very prescriptive and didactic teaching that inhibits the quality of the learning within PE. The National Physical Education, School Sport and Clubs Links (PESSCL) strategy (2003) has supported the development of a model to illustrate *High Quality Physical Education and School Sport.* Integral to this model is the significance of effective teaching and learning. What is stressed is the importance of the teacher's role in understanding how to plan appropriately to meet children's needs and to design and deliver appropriate learning opportunities which support effective organisation and safe practice. This requires teachers to understand what they are teaching and how to bring about learning within PE. Knowledge of the *what* and the *how* requires reflective practice and engagement with professional development opportunities where there are opportunities for engaging with up-to-date debates and an appraisal of practice. How we teach and bring about learning involves questioning our approach to practice. As many aspects of safety are implicit within PE pedagogy, this requires teachers to rehearse fundamental questions relating to preparation and planning for learning. As Bailey and Macfayden (2000: 14) identify planning also involves 'a myriad of less obvious aspects: leading children into the physical education area; changing between tasks; arranging groups; spotting potential problems before they arise; and so on'.

Implicit within promoting *high quality* PE, (PESSCL, 2003) is the importance of:

- preparation and developing subject knowledge;
- learning that is appropriately challenging without inhibiting learners;
- lessons that are appropriately tailored to meet learning needs;
- engaging learners in a range of teaching styles;
- appropriate deployment of support staff and resources;
- engaging learners through assessment for learning;
- safe practice in preparing for and engaging in PE.

Preparation involves clear reference to what is to be taught and how learning is approached. The range of subject knowledge required to teach effectively and safely within the primary PE curriculum requires teachers to operate from well-planned schemes of work and lesson planning that encompass children's individual learning needs. An important aspect of teaching safely is that the pitch of the lesson is appropriate, and that the teacher has the required knowledge to execute the lesson. This demands careful planning and updating knowledge and understanding over time.

Making safety principles explicit within lesson preparation

An important element of safe practice is teachers' awareness of the general teaching and organisation requirements for physical education lessons. It is important for you as a teacher to consider the complexity of the endeavour in terms of the requirements for the specific activity areas within PE and the variation in the management and organisation of the varied learning contexts. It is also important that teachers work within their knowledge base and consider within NCPE the different strands of physical education within the curriculum. Increasingly, there are opportunities for teachers to update their knowledge (as noted in Chapter 3) through CPD opportunities. Whatever is being taught, however, must only include activities that teachers are competent to teach safely.

The specific teaching considerations

It is vital for teachers to consider the key contextual and location factors that will influence lessons.

- The space or context where the lesson is taking place.
- The specific teaching considerations that need to be checked (e.g. playground, off-site area, movement hall).
- That the apparatus and equipment to be used are in good condition and are fit for purpose.
- The Health and Safety Policy and operating procedures for PE.

The pitch of the lesson content – matching the child to the content

Establishing what the children are capable of undertaking and ensuring that tasks are not too challenging are both essential for safe practice. Teachers need to ensure the following:

- their own knowledge of the class and the extent of that knowledge. What assessments should inform their planning? What information do teachers use to understand the learning needs of children that will in turn influence planning?
- They devise appropriate tasks that reflect levels of progression within them.
- They match children's capabilities to the tasks being set.

Planning for children with Special Educational Needs

Teachers needs to ensure that they are familiar with the policy for Special Educational Needs. Children's needs will be varied and may arise as a direct result of participating in physical activity because they have specific medical condition e.g. diabetes, asthma, eczema. Children may also have specific impairments such as sensory impairments (e.g. a hearing or sight impairment) or medical impairments (e.g. epilepsy) or physical impairment (e.g. an artificial limb). Specific emotional or behavioural needs will also need to be clearly understood. Considering how these varied needs might be accommodated will require a teacher to work with the SENCO and the parents of the children in order that the activity might best be safely adapted to meet their needs. Other considerations such as monitoring children in the class, communicating with children during the lesson and supporting children participation will all need to be carefully planned.

Children's awareness of safety

Consideration as to how the children are prepared for and involved in decision-making about safety requires a teacher to reflect on what routines are important to build into the lesson. From an early age children should be engaged in this process through teachers establishing clear protocols within teaching.

Communicating and reporting sickness

Primary children can be very sensitive to changing conditions and this can impact on their capacity to participate. Young children warm up quickly but can also cool down quickly, which means they are more susceptible to changes within the environment. The teachers need to be aware of this and encourage children to report if they feel unwell, dizzy, sick, cold or overheated. The conditions for safe participation e.g. hydration, sunburn, or cold, are also important to bear in mind.

Clothing

Teachers need to share with children what is appropriate clothing for PE. Modelling this through their own dress code is extremely important. Key features that need to be considered include the following:

- What is suitable for the activity should be communicated through the school's PE policy.
- Footware – reflecting on why wearing socks or normal shoes would be unsuitable.
- Establishing safety habits e.g. tying hair back and the removal of jewellery.
- The hygiene principles relating to changing for PE.

First Aid and emergency procedures

Teachers need to be clear about the course of action they need to take in the event of an injury. These include:

- The school procedures in the event of an accident, including the nominated person responsible for First Aid.
- The location of the First Aid kit.
- How an accident is reported and followed up, including the completion of an accident report form.

Organisation

Teachers need to make decisions about how the learning will be organised and about the specific organisational routines that will be implemented: how children will be grouped for activities, how transition points will be managed, the organisation of equipment within a lesson. Crucial to establishing safety is visualising the lesson, its activities, its structure, and how it will be delivered (Bailey and Macfayden, 2000).

- Establishing clear routines for changing and within these ensuring that children are safe to participate. This includes controlled movement from the classroom to the activity area.
- Clear communication relating to expectations at the start of and throughout a lesson.
- Clear signals for starting and stopping activities and the children responding readily to instructions.
- Well-thought-through organisational routines, including setting up the space and the movement of equipment, apparatus and children.
- Clear routines for identifying safety and risk e.g. children participating with the teacher in checking clothing and equipment.
- Clear routines for reflecting on the principles of safety e.g. lifting and carrying and warming up and cooling down.

Principles for good practice in lesson preparation

Focus on principles for safe practice. Use the checklist below to support your lesson reflection.

1. Lessons are pre-empted by a controlled changing session prior to entering the workspace
- Have the children been alerted to what they will be doing during the pending lesson?
- Have they been asked to immediately set about an activity on entering the workspace?
- Have the mood and tone of the lesson been set even before the children enter the workspace?
- Such detail should be noted in the lesson plan for the session.

2. A set format is followed for the delivery of the lesson
- Warm-up, movement content e.g. skills practice and application including evaluation, and cool down activity.
- Are the children engaged in planning, performing and evaluating within their learning?
- Are the children challenged by the content?
- Do they have opportunities to watch others and are they invited to comment on each other's work?
- Is a range of demonstration strategies applied within the session (individual children, pairs, groups, half the class, teacher)?
- Are issues related to health, safety and hygiene addressed within the session?
- Do children have opportunities to work individually, in pairs, in small groups?
- Is there visible evidence to note progression in the work, building on prior knowledge and experience and leading to improvement of the work?
- Is a variation in teaching style evident?

3. A wide variety of equipment and resources is available (and used) in sessions
- Do these support learning across the range of abilities?
- Is provision made for individual needs and are resources suitably differentiated?
- Are areas allocated for work and clearly defined for the children (boundaries marked, etc.)?
- Are the children aware of the potential (and safe) usage of the equipment?
- Are they encouraged to make their own decisions on how best to use the equipment to enable a level of

success to surface prior to technical input?

- Are they instructed in working safely with due regard to others and handling equipment correctly?
- Do they display an ability to take growing responsibility for their own and others' safety?

4. Lessons are satisfactorily concluded

- When appropriate a satisfactory (physical) cool down is included.
- There is follow-up of work done during the session through verbal discussion and a review of work covered.
- Highlighted areas to work on in future lessons are noted.
- The children are asked to comment on how things went, to identify aspects of their work they feel were improved on and those that need further consolidation and practice.
- Were the children asked about how they felt about the session?
- Did they enjoy the activities?
- What specifically did they like/dislike about the session?
- What have they learnt from it?

REFLECTIVE TASK

Arrange to conduct observations of PE lessons across the school in consultation with the PE coordinator. Use the *principles for good practice in lesson preparation* above to reflect on the range of lessons. Make notes under each key heading that can be shared with the teachers and the coordinator. What areas from your observations can you recognise as good practice and what areas need to be discussed?

The management of the environment

Managing the environment is a key component of safety within physical education. Having a safe and orderly environment is paramount with PE lessons. This involves the management of facilities and equipment and considering how these are prepared and managed within PE lessons. The school's PE policy should include resource management, as well as the maintenance and replacement of equipment and should give clear guidance for teachers on the routines and procedures for safe operation during the lesson.

The varied contexts that are utilised within PE, including indoor and outdoor, large and small apparatus, and movement and seasonal variations require teachers to be diligent at all times to ensure that the environment remains fit for purpose. The effective care and maintenance of the physical space, equipment, and the storage and use are all key to the maintenance of a safe environment. A typical primary school will not have a dedicated movement hall and therefore the teacher must ensure that the space remains free from hazards and that equipment in open access areas does not become damaged. As Severs et al. (2003) highlight it is vital for equipment to be inspected annually by a specialist company. Ultimately, schools are responsible for ensuring that inspections take place and equipment is monitored. The range of equipment available for PE and its specificity does require that any repairs that might be undertaken will require a specialist. Listed below are some of the typical checks the teachers would make within specific areas of the PE curriculum. This list is not extensive and it is important that the BAALPE (2004) guidance is the key reference point here.

Gymnastics

Typically, teachers will need to consider the following before a lesson.

The floor
This needs to be clean, non-slip and free from damage. Ideally, it should also be sprung to support safe landings.

Small apparatus
This includes gymnastic mats and everything here should be in good condition. Teachers need to check that equipment is stable and free from damage.

- Surfaces and coverings should be free from tears and other damage.
- Rubber feet that provide stability for equipment, such as stools, A frames, benches and gymnastic tables must be intact and the equipment should be stable.
- Hooks and attachments should be secure and in good working order.
- Mats must be the appropriate size, weight and thickness for the age of the children.
- Wooden equipment such as gymnastics benches and planks must be splinter free.

Large or fixed apparatus
This includes large climbing frames, bars and beams. Teachers will need to consider the following.

- How is the equipment secured? A teacher will need to check the mechanisms are working effectively e.g. bolts, tensioning wires, locking devices and the overall general stability of the equipment.

Dance

Typically a teacher will need to consider the following before a lesson.

The floor
As with gymnastics, the floor needs to be clean, non-slip and free from damage. Ideally it should also be sprung to support safe landings.

Typically the equipment for dance will involve the teacher checking the following.

- Music equipment – how it is positioned so that cables are not a hazard.
- Visual equipment – stands and connecting wires.
- Musical instruments – must be safe to use and in good condition.
- Props – masks or other props must be appropriate for use and should not put children at risk.

Games

Typically, a teacher will need to consider the following before a lesson.

The playing area

Check that surfaces are in good condition and there are no trip hazards or uneven areas/ breakage. A teacher should also check indoor and outdoor surfaces regularly for cleanliness, wear and tear and general build-up. Indoor areas need to be checked to ensure that the space is free from obstacles, equipment and fixtures that are placed in the hall between lessons. Almost all indoor hall spaces are used for more than one purpose and the teacher will need to remove all hazards prior to the lesson.

Outdoor spaces such as the playground
These will be prone to seasonal change. Commonly, leaves, moss, and wet conditions can create changes to an outdoor surface. The teacher must be diligent and aware of the changing conditions and the potential hazards. Playing fields and grass areas also need to be checked for hazards such as glass or other objects.

Equipment for games lessons
This will tend to fall into two categories.

- Small, portable apparatus like bats, balls, bean bags, markers, hoops, quoits etc. Equipment should be in good condition and fit for purpose. It also needs to be transported safely to and from the lesson in nets or carrying crates as appropriate and no one and should carry items individually. Ideally the distribution of equipment should happen where the lesson is to take place.
- Large equipment which should be checked for wear and tear and stability. Posts, nets, goals are all items that would normally be moved under the supervision of the teacher. Correct lifting and carrying will be essential when lifting any items and children should be taught the correct techniques.

Athletics

Typically, a teacher will need to consider the following before a lesson.

As with games the teacher will need to check indoor and outdoor surfaces and playing fields are in good condition and surfaces are free from hazards and appropriate for use.

Equipment for primary athletics
This will tend to fall into two categories.

- Small apparatus – for throwing e.g. balls, bean bags, quoits, shuttlecocks.
- Specialist equipment for primary use e.g. foam javelins, foam-covered light-weight discus and shot putts. Other equipment such as discs, markers, canes and cones may be also used.

Gymnastics mats
These as required for landing areas for standing jumps.

Establishing suitable areas for throwing will also need to be considered including how the environment can be organised to support slinging and putting and ensure the safety of other groups working within the same environment.

Outdoor and adventurous activities

Typically, a teacher will need to consider the following before a lesson.

The location, whether it is indoors or on the school site or in a familiar place. As with games, the locations will need to be checked by the teacher who, in addition, will need to undertake a risk assessment in order to manage the potential risks activities might pose, for example groupings for undertaking problem-based challenges and children being out of sight to undertake tasks on the school grounds (like orienteering). Safety is paramount and a teacher should only select activities that are within children's capabilities, knowledge and expertise. Any equipment should be checked prior to being used and if it is set up prior to the lesson e.g. a parachute, will need to be checked before the children begin the activity. Teachers must also be aware of the correct procedures for lifting and carrying and provide clear instructions on how these should be undertaken.

Using a specialist centre for outdoor and adventurous activities

As noted earlier in this chapter the duty of care ultimately rests with teachers. It is essential that thorough planning and preparation are undertaken with respect to the suitability of a centre and its compliance with the health and safety requirements. Woodhouse (2003: 119) lists seven key factors that are important for the teacher to check.

- Their Health and Safety Policy and code of practice.
- Public liability insurance.
- Possession of a current licence from the Adventure Activity Licensing Authority (check all the activities are mentioned).
- Qualifications and experience of the staff.
- Any independent recognition or accreditation e.g. British Canoe Union (BCU).
- Condition of equipment.
- First Aid provision and the accessibility of doctors and hospital facilities.

Other important considerations that will need to be discussed are:
- CRB clearance of all personnel at an off-site location.
- Children/adult ratios for activities.
- Male and female staff supporting off-site activities.

Swimming

Typically, a teacher will need to consider the following before a lesson.

Swimming pool sites by law must have a Safety Policy. It is important for teachers to check the procedures for pool safety, including the procedure for changing and emergencies. As noted in the section above on duty of care, a teacher is always responsible for their class and the overall conduct of the lesson. Careful checks must be made relating to the deployment of specialist staff (swimming instructors and life guards) and the definition of their roles. A thorough risk assessment must be undertaken to ensure that consideration is given to the location, organisational requirements and the procedures for safety at the swimming pool and conduct for lessons. Important considerations for the teacher to check include the following.

- The Health and Safety Policy including the emergency and operating procedures.
- Qualifications and experience of the staff.
- Policy on pupil/teacher ratios.
- Pre-instruction and preparation in school before going swimming for the first time, including an awareness of children's individual needs and the clear identification of these needs. It may be necessary to identify children quickly e.g. through them wearing different coloured swimming hats.
- Operational procedures, including routines from the changing area to the pool; procedure on the pool side; hygiene; on-going safety routines e.g. counting pupils, entry and exit from the pool, signs and signals and how to respond in an emergency.
- First Aid provision and safety equipment.

Other important considerations that will need to be discussed are:
- CRB clearance of all staff/supporting adults including volunteers accompanying swimming groups.
- Children/adult ratios for activities.
- Male and female staff supporting off-site activities.

Developing safe management within PE lessons

Preparation and planning are key to ensuring that teachers implement safety principles prior to the delivery of PE lessons. The school PE policy sets important expectations concerning working procedures and teachers should be aware of these safety principles when undertaking lessons. The operationalisation of lessons will typically consider seven key elements.

- The clarity of the lesson objectives and of the key movement tasks.
- How the lesson will be delivered – the teaching style.
- The organisation of learning including the grouping of children in light of individual needs.
- Communication, including key language and feedback.
- The routines to be established e.g. changing, handling apparatus and transitions from the classroom to the space to the movement hall.
- The organisation of equipment storage and handling and the management of apparatus during the lesson.
- The key principles of safety e.g. warming up and cooling down, lifting and carrying, rules for participation, signals.

As each of the areas of activity have specific considerations, the BAALPE (2004) guidance provides detailed information and clear reference points which are important for teachers to access. This section will highlight some general considerations for gymnastics, dance, games. Lesson delivery for each of the areas of activity would typically reflect on the following.

Gymnastics

- The theme for the lesson and the key actions and skills to be developed referenced to the school scheme of work – including key instructions and vocabulary.
- Movement tasks should be devised so they can be accessed by children working at a range of levels. The tasks show progression through the lesson.
- Teaching method should be linked to the lesson objective and teachers need to be clear about the expectations for different aspects of the lesson.
- The organisation of children – for floor and apparatus work which needs to be linked to individual needs.
- The organisation of equipment and resources – developing an apparatus plan with a clear layout, including how it will be moved, where it will be positioned and how it will be checked after it has been set up.
- Key principles for safety, including signals for starting and stopping, warming up and cooling down, lifting and carrying, assembling apparatus, checking apparatus, storage.

Dance

- The stimuli for the lesson and the key actions and dynamics that will be developed should be referenced to the school scheme of work, including key instructions and vocabulary.
- Developing movement tasks that provide the children with opportunities to experience composition, performance and appreciation and to select and refine elements of their work.
- The teaching method should be linked to the lesson objective and the teacher needs to be clear about the

expectations for different aspects of the lesson.

- The organisation of children within the space (individually or in groups) and the spatial pathways and movement around the space.
- The organisation of equipment and resources within the lesson. How props will be introduced and any specific instructions on how to use equipment.
- Key principles for safety, including signals for starting and stopping, warming up and cooling down, carrying and storage of objects.

Games

- The theme for the lesson (invasion, net-wall, striking and fielding) and the actions and skills to be developed (sending, receiving and travelling skills) referenced to the school scheme of work, including key instructions and vocabulary.
- Movement tasks should be devised so that they can be accessed by children working at a range of levels. The tasks show the development of skill, movement and strategy through the progression through the lesson.
- Teaching method which should be linked to the lesson objective – teachers need to be clear about the expectations for different aspects of the lesson.
- The organisation of children in relation to grouping, the direction of objects, and movement needs to be linked to individual needs.
- The organisation of equipment and resources by developing a plan for the playing area with layouts for paired and group aspects of the lesson. The distribution and collection of equipment through the lesson would normally be managed in smaller groups and commonly colour-coded.
- Key principles for safety including signals for starting and stopping, warming up and cooling down, lifting and carrying, handling objects, and directional aspects of play. moving within the playing areas would also be featured.

Athletics

- The theme for the lesson (running, jumping, throwing, or a combined theme) and skills to be developed within each aspect e.g. running for speed, distance, varying pace; jumping – for distance or height; throwing overarm, underarm, round arm). The content needs to be referenced to the school scheme of work, including key instructions and vocabulary.
- Movement tasks should be devised so that they can be accessed by children working at a range of levels. The tasks show the development of skill and progression through the lesson.
- Teaching method which should be linked to the lesson objective – teachers need to be clear about the expectations for different aspects of the lesson.
- The organisation of children in relation to grouping and the direction of the activities which need to be linked to individual needs.
- The organisation of equipment and resources by developing a plan of the area indicating throwing areas with a throwing line and coned safe areas. Layouts for of the lesson should be clearly marked on the plan.
- The distribution and collection of equipment throughout the lesson and keeping within specific zones would both need to be stressed.
- Key principles for safety, including signals for starting and stopping, warming up and cooling down, lifting and carrying and handling objects. Directional zoning would also need be emphasised.

Outdoor and Adventurous Activities

- The theme for the lesson with a key focus (e.g. problem solving, cooperation, trust, orienteering) and the skills and process to be developed within each aspect. The content needs to be referenced to the school scheme of work, including key instructions and vocabulary.

- The tasks should be devised so they can be accessed by children working at a range of levels. The teaching method should be linked to the lesson objective and teachers need to be clear about the expectations for different aspects of the lesson.
- The organisation of children in relation to grouping, and the nature of the activity needs to be linked to individual needs.
- The organisation of equipment and resources developing a plan of the area indicating the layout.
- The distribution and collection of equipment throughout the lesson.
- Key principles for safety including conducting a risk assessment (for activities on- and off-site), signals for starting and stopping, warming up and cooling down, and lifting and carrying and handling objects.

Swimming

- The theme for the lesson has a key focus. Content would be typically developed under three key themes (confidence, propulsion and water safety). The content needs to be referenced to the school scheme of work, including key instructions and vocabulary.
- The tasks should be devised so they are accessible and clear for all the children participating.
- Teaching method.
- The organisation of children – pupil/teacher ratios and routines in relation to grouping e.g. buddy systems. The nature of the activity should be linked to individual needs.
- The organisation of equipment and resources – developing a plan of the pool layout indicating areas and movement (shallow and deep areas, entry and exit points and the location of life guards).
- The distribution and collection of equipment through the lesson – floats and aids and goggles.
- Key principles for safety, including conducting a risk assessment pre-instruction (including children's awareness of the environment and its dangers and specifics on hygiene and routines, assembly points, etc.). Communication should include signals (both manual and verbal), starting and stopping, and emergency procedures.

REFLECTIVE TASK

Consider the management of resources in your school and reflect on the following:

- What resources are available within each area of PE?
- Is there a policy for checking equipment and for replacing faulty equipment?
- Are there sufficient resources to support effective delivery of the curriculum?
- Are the resources appropriate for the activities?

PRACTICAL TASK PRACTICAL TASK PRACTICAL TASK PRACTICAL TASK PRACTICAL TASK

Ask yourself the following key questions.

- Can you identify the key responsibilities of your school with respect to health and safety?
- What is meant by duty of care?
- What are the key factors which contribute to safe practice?
- What key safety guidance for physical education is it important to have access to?

A SUMMARY OF **KEY POINTS**

This chapter has reflected on important aspects of safe practice with primary Physical Education. It has also examined important safety processes as part of whole school policy and considered the teacher's duty of care in a changing context where instructors and sports coaches are increasingly involved in the delivery of PE lessons. Importantly, key considerations for the primary teacher have been highlighted with respect to lesson preparation and delivery. This chapter has also stressed the key characteristics and features of safe practice referenced to the BAALPE (2004) guidelines and the Association for Physical Education (2007) Guidelines for Good Practice. Safe practice as illustrated in this chapter is an integral part of learning within physical education.

REFERENCES REFERENCES **REFERENCES** REFERENCES **REFERENCES** REFERENCES

AfPE (2007). *Best Practice Guidance*

Bailey, R. and Macfayden, T. (2000). *Teaching Physical Education 5–11*. London: Continuum.

BAALPE (2004).

DfCSF (2007) 'Teaching in England. Care and Safety of Pupils'. Available at www.teachernet.gov.uk

Pickup, I. and Price, L. (2007) *Teaching Physical Education in the Primary School*. London: Continuum.

Raymond, C. (1998). *Coordinating Physical Education Across the Primary School*. Abingdon: Falmer.

Severs, J.,Whitlam, P. and Woodhouse, J. (2003). *Safety and Risk Assessment in Primary School Physical Education*. Abingdon: Routledge.

The National Physical Education, School Sport and Clubs Links (PESSCL) strategy

TDA (2007) *The Revised Standards for the Recommendation for Qualified Teacher Status (QTS)*. London: TDA.

FURTHER READING FURTHER READING **FURTHER READING** FURTHER READING

Bailey, R. (2001) *Teaching Physical Education – A Handbook for Primary and Secondary School Teachers*. London: Kogan Page.

DfEE (1999) *Physical Education in the National Curriculum*. London: DfEE and QCA.

DfES (2000) *Curriculum Guidance for the Foundation Stage*. London: DfES and QCA.

Williams, A. (ed.) (2000) *Primary School Physical Education: Research into Practice*. Abingdon: Routledge.

Appendix
Professional standards for QTS: examples of trainee practice in physical education

1. PROFESSIONAL ATTRIBUTES	Example of trainee practice in physical education
Q1. Have high expectations of children and young people and a commitment to ensuring that they can achieve their full educational potential and to establishing fair, respectful, trusting, supportive and constructive relationships with them.	A trainee volunteers to accompany his Key Stage 2 class on a residential Outdoor Adventurous Activities trip. He works alongside the subject leader, class teacher and centre staff and parents to clarify expectations for children's learning during this trip and uses the experience to develop trusting, supportive and constructive relationships with the children.
Q2. Demonstrate the positive values, attitudes and behaviour they expect from children and young people.	A trainee shows enthusiasm by changing into PE kit for lessons and ensures that learning is at the heart of every PE lesson through detailed planning.
Q3. (a) Be aware of the professional duties of teachers and the statutory framework within which they work. (b) Be aware of the policies and practices of the workloads and share in collective responsibility for their implementation.	A trainee meets with the PE subject leader to clarify the PE Health and Safety Policy. She is especially concerned with teaching off-site (games activities are usually taught in the local park) and after reading current recommendations (BAALPE), carries out a risk assessment for the upcoming block of work.
Q4. Communicate effectively with children, young people, colleagues, parents and carers.	After speaking with the headteacher, a trainee uses the school intranet website to celebrate the work of his Year 4 class during the spring term. Examples of pupils' peer-assessments are uploaded to the site and shared with colleagues who use the information to inform future planning.
Q5. Recognise and respect the contribution that colleagues, parents and carers can make to the development and well-being of children and young people and to raising their levels of attainment.	A trainee asks parents and carers to suggest ideas and materials that could be used as starting points for dance activities during the autumn term. At the end of the unit of work, the same parents and carers are invited into school to celebrate the achievements of their children.
Q6. Have a commitment to collaboration and cooperative working.	During teaching practice, a trainee works as part of the whole-school team to plan and facilitate 'sports day'. She ensures that all the children in her class can participate in the event and creates a programme for the day using her desktop publishing skills.

Q7. (a) Reflect on and improve their practice, and take responsibility for identifying and meeting their developing professional needs. (b) Identify priorities for their early professional development in the context of induction.	Following a limited exposure to the PE curriculum during Stage 1 teaching practice, a trainee identifies the need to gain experience in teaching gymnastic activities. She negotiates an opportunity to plan, teach and assess a sequence of linked lessons and to apply knowledge acquired in a recent college-based course. The same trainee identifies that professional development during the induction year is important and – following appointment to post – makes an early contact with the local Lead Development Agency in order to access CPD courses.
Q8. Have a creative and constructively critical approach towards innovation, being prepared to adapt their practice where benefits and improvements are identified.	A trainee attends a whole-school INSET course that is delivered by a local authority lead trainer. The course examines inclusion in PE and the trainee seeks to apply the strategies introduced in the course within her teaching. She is especially keen to explore ways of engaging the most-able children and begins to use ICT to support pupils' work in the evaluate and improve aspect of NCPE.
Q9. Act upon advice and feedback and be open to coaching and mentoring.	Following a 'satisfactory' PE lesson, a trainee acts on feedback from the school experience mentor (who observed the lesson) to try and improve specific aspects. In particular the assessment and recording of pupils' learning are an agreed focus for the next lesson in sequence and the trainee creates an assessment grid that is clearly linked to the stated learning intentions.

2. PROFESSIONAL KNOWLEDGE AND UNDERSTANDING	**Example of trainee practice in physical education**
Q10. Have a knowledge and understanding of a range of teaching, learning and behaviour management strategies and know how to use and adapt them, including how to personalise learning and provide opportunities for all learners to achieve their potential.	Having made some initial observations and assessments of pupils' work in PE, a trainee plans carefully differentiated tasks within a games activities lesson which focus on invasion games. Tasks are set for different groups of children and variation is achieved by using different equipment, space and numbers in teams.

Q11. Know the assessment requirements and arrangements for the subjects/ curriculum areas they are trained to teach, including those relating to public examinations and qualifications.	A trainee proactively seeks opportunities to work alongside class teachers who are preparing end of term reports for pupils. Although he finds this demanding, the ensuing discussion with class teachers is valuable and informative to all. In particular, comments based on the 'four aspects' of NCPE are included in each pupil's report.
Q12. Know a range of approaches to assessment, including the importance of formative assessment.	A final stage trainee uses a system of 'formative assessment' during a six week series of dance activities with a Year 5 class. By the end of the unit of work, each pupil has collected a range of photographs, skill analysis grids, video clips and peer-assessment information. The trainee meets with the class teacher to discuss how this information can be used to inform subsequent planning.
Q13. Know how to use local and national statistical information to evaluate the effectiveness of their teaching, to monitor the progress of those they teach and to raise levels of attainment.	A trainee uses information provided by the local authority regarding children's attainment in 'physical development' at the end of the Early Years Foundation Stage to plan and assess her pupils' work in a Year 1 class. She thinks that the majority of pupils are exceeding expectations and plans tasks that will continue to provide appropriate challenge.
Q14 Have a secure knowledge and understanding of their subjects/curriculum areas and related pedagogy to enable them to teach effectively across the age and ability range for which they are trained to teach.	A trainee works with school- and college-based staff to ensure that (over the duration of her undergraduate degree) she gains practical experience within games, gymnastics and dance activities. She also completes a written PE assignment in the second year of her course which focuses on the 'acquire and develop' aspect of NCPE.
Q15. Know and understand the relevant statutory and non-statutory curricula and frameworks, including those provided through the National Strategies, for their subjects/curriculum areas, and other relevant initiatives applicable to the age and ability range for which they are trained.	A trainee works alongside the class teacher and other colleagues to ensure that the national PSA target of two hours per week of high-quality PE and sport is achieved for her pupils. She also seeks to make connections between PE and other subjects and encourages children's creative skills through the teaching of literacy alongside dance activities.
Q16. Have passed the professional skills tests in numeracy, literacy and information and communication technology (ICT).	

Q17. Know how to use skills in literacy, numeracy and ICT to support their teaching and wider professional activities.	A trainee uses a variety of simple software packages to manage his own plans and records of pupils' work. He uses a database to keep a record of formative assessments in physical education, linked to NCPE level descriptors, which is shared with other colleagues to help them plan for individual needs.
Q18. Understand how children and young people develop and that the progress and well-being of learners are affected by a range of developmental, social, religious, ethnic, cultural and linguistic influences.	By taking a 'developmental approach', a trainee plans tasks in PE that are specifically matched to meet individual needs. During a teaching practice, the class includes children from a variety of ethnic groups; the trainee draws on this aspect to support learning in dance activities by drawing on a wide range of cultural influences.
Q19. Know how to make effective personalised provision for those they teach, including those for whom English is an additional language or who have special educational needs, and how to take practical account of diversity and promote equality and inclusion in their teaching.	A trainee focuses on using task cards to 'scaffold' children's learning in swimming activities and for water safety. For some children in the Year 2 class English is an additional language, and the trainee works with the TA to use two languages on each card.
Q20. Know and understand the roles of colleagues with specific responsibilities, including those with responsibility for learners with special educational needs and disabilities and other individual learning needs.	A trainee meets with the SENCO to discuss policy and practice with particular reference to the pupil in her class identified with ADHD. The trainee is particularly concerned that PE experiences can build on this child's seemingly limitless desire to move whilst not compromising safety for the whole class.
Q21. (a) Be aware of current legal requirements, national policies and guidance on the safeguarding and promotion of well-being of children and young people.	A trainee completes a college-based directed task that shows how the five outcomes of *Every Child Matters* link to National Curriculum requirements in Key Stage 1. She attempts to reflect this in her teaching of PE and specifically includes learning intentions that relate to health and the fostering of self-esteem among the children by using meaningful and enjoyable activities.
(b) Know how to identify and support children and young people whose progress, development or well-being is affected by changes or difficulties in their personal circumstances, and when to refer them to colleagues for specialist support.	A trainee is concerned that an 8 year old child in her class suddenly appears to have little energy and struggles to remain active in PE for sustained periods of time. The trainee consults with the class teacher who in turn speaks with the headteacher and an associated health professional; in collaboration with the pupil's parents, guidance is offered concerning dietary intake and sleep requirements.

3. PROFESSIONAL SKILLS	Example of trainee practice in physical education
Q22. Plan for progression across the age and ability range for which they are trained, designing effective learning sequences within lessons and across series of lessons and demonstrating secure subject/ curriculum knowledge.	A student in her final stage of ITT seeks an opportunity to plan, teach and assess a sequence of lessons in Athletics Activities. She finds out the level of prior experience in this activity area and attempts to map out a unit of work that will challenge her Year 5 pupils. In her planning, she identifies clear learning intentions which will extend the pupils' knowledge and understanding to include new and different ways of throwing a range of objects for distance and accuracy.
Q23. Design opportunities for learners to develop their literacy, numeracy and ICT skills.	Following a gymnastics activities lesson with a Year 2 class, a trainee uses video clips of the pupils moving to focus on movement vocabulary. The pupils use the interactive whiteboard in the classroom to suggest appropriate words that are then written next to still images of their actions.
Q24. Plan homework or other out-of-class work to sustain learners' progress and to extend and consolidate their learning.	A trainee uses questioning during a PE warm up to check pupils' understanding about the short-term effects of exercise on the body. She uses existing knowledge to link with on-going work in Science and asks children to measure heart rates across a normal day, including their time at home and before and after school. She helps the children to create a heart rate log and uses these data, in particular data gathered over a weekend, during maths lessons.
Q25. Teach lessons and sequences of lessons across the age and ability range for which they are trained in which they: (a) use a range of teaching strategies and resources, including e-learning, taking practical account of diversity and promoting equality and inclusion.	Despite initial concerns regarding maintaining control of the pupils, a trainee adopts a 'guided discovery' style when teaching a floorwork gymnastics activity in Key Stage 2. She prepares task cards to engage the pupils in the planning and evaluation of their own work.
(b) build on prior knowledge, develop concepts and processes, enable learners to apply new knowledge, understanding and skills and meet learning objectives.	During a placement with a Year 4 class, a trainee uses the knowledge accrued by pupils in a concurrent sequence of geography lessons to good effect in an Outdoor and Adventurous Activities context. The trainee plans activities where the pupils can apply navigation skills in teams, within the school grounds, in a variety of orienteering challenges.

(c) adapt their language to suit the learners they teach, introducing new ideas and concepts clearly, and using explanations, questions, discussions and plenaries effectively.	During a dance activities lesson, a trainee works with a small group of Year 1 pupils to explore the use of space. The trainee is surprised at how quickly the children are able to work skilfully in their own space and extends the pupils' learning by introducing partner and trio work. The trainee uses discussion to prompt the pupils to work at different levels and to complement each other's work. The trainee asks the children to demonstrate their work to the rest of the class during the plenary and asks the observers to suggest what they like about the observed actions.
(d) demonstrate the ability to manage learning of individuals, groups and whole classes, modifying their teaching to suit the stage of the lesson.	A trainee uses 'exploration' and 'guided discovery' teaching styles to engage the whole class at the start of a games activity lesson. As the lesson progresses, the trainee provides individuals and small groups with appropriate and specific feedback whilst maintaining a careful watch over the whole class.
Q26. (c) Make effective use of a range of assessment, monitoring and recording strategies.	A trainee uses principles of assessment for learning to design four systems for assessing and recording pupils' progress in gymnastics activities. Simple formats for individual, group, peer- and self-assessment are used across a unit of work to create a portfolio of achievement.
(b) Assess the learning needs of those they teach in order to set challenging learning objectives.	During the early stages of school-based practice, a trainee observes Year 3 pupils working in a games activity context. It is evident that many pupils are unable to demonstrate a range of sending and receiving skills and that some are restricted by competitive practices. The trainee plans the following lesson to include differentiated tasks and to allow all pupils more time and space 'on the ball'.
Q27. Provide timely, accurate and constructive feedback on learners' attainment, progress and areas for development.	A trainee plans a Year 1 PE lesson with a learning intention of 'acquiring and developing sending and receiving skills'. At the planning stage, she thinks through the appropriate movement vocabulary required to give instructions and provide feedback. During the lesson the trainee uses this language (using a prompt card to remind her) to give constructive feedback, particularly in relation to body position and arm action within ball rolling and throwing actions for accuracy.

Q28. Support and guide learners to reflect on their learning, identify the progress they have made and identify their emerging learning needs.	A trainee uses questioning to check pupils' understanding within the main activity in a Year 6 Athletics Activities lesson (the lesson is focusing on evaluating and improving each other's work in running activities). She challenges the pupils to analyse travelling actions and to consider the changes to technique that can be made to cover various distances in less time. Each child completes a self-assessment log that includes a focus for subsequent lessons.
Q29. Evaluate the impact of their teaching on the progress of all learners, and modify their planning and classroom practice where necessary.	A trainee evaluates all lessons, including those in PE. In the early stages of ITT, these comments reflect largely on health and safety and behaviour management issues. As the trainee becomes more experienced in teaching PE, evaluations become more focused on quality of learning and small changes that can be made to strengthen the experience of each child.
Q30. Establish a purposeful and safe learning environment conducive to learning and identify opportunities for learners to learn in out-of-school contexts.	A trainee follows school-based and national best practice guidelines for health and safety in PE. He involves the children in preparing a health and safety poster for the upcoming unit of work taking place in a swimming pool at a local sports centre and prepares laminated resource cards that provide visual learning stimuli.
Q31. Establish a clear framework for classroom discipline to manage learners' behaviour constructively and promote their self-control and independence.	A trainee who is working with a Year 2 class is concerned about the children becoming boisterous during gymnastics activities in the school hall. She sets early learning tasks that emphasise control, accuracy and neatness of body actions and encourages each child to work in their own defined space (initially using individual mats and hoops as a guide).
Q32. Work as a team member and identify opportunities for working with colleagues, sharing the development of effective practice with them.	A trainee attends a whole-school INSET course that is delivered by a local authority lead trainer. The course examines inclusion in PE and the trainee seeks to apply the strategies introduced in the course within her teaching. She is especially keen to find ways of engaging the most-able children and begins to use ICT to support pupils' work in the evaluate and improve aspect of NCPE. This is successful and she is asked to feedback to colleagues at the end-of-term staff meeting.
Q33. Ensure that colleagues working with them are appropriately involved in supporting learning and understand the roles they are expected to fulfil.	A trainee makes effective use of her teaching assistant (TA) in PE. During a unit of work in dance activities, the TA scaffolds pupils' work with appropriate feedback and feed forward, using movement vocabulary that the trainee has written on a prompt card and discussed before the lesson.

Adapted from: Pickup, I. and Price. L. (2007) *Teaching Physical Education in the Primary School: A Developmental Approach*. London: Continuum.